The Idle Angler

The Idle Angler

Kevin Parr

ELLESMERE
THE MEDLAR PRESS
2014

Published by The Medlar Press Limited,
The Grange, Ellesmere, Shropshire.
www.medlarpress.com

ISBN 978-1-907110-47-4

Produced in England by The Medlar Press Limited, Ellesmere.
Designed and typeset in 11 on 13$^{1}/_{2}$pt Garamond.

Contents

To my parents - for their love,
patience and lifts to
the lakes . . .

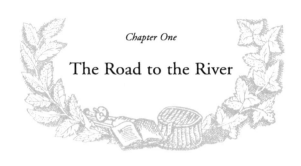

Chapter One

The Road to the River

All journeys have secret destinations of which the traveller is unaware.
MARK TWAIN

In an ideal world, we would all live in cosy cottages with a chalk-stream sparkling across the bottom of the garden and a lily filled lake tucked into the trees further down the valley.

We would have spacious hallways with rods already made up and whenever the need took us, we would stroll out of the door and cast a line.

We would catch trout in the spring, carp and tench in the summer, perch and roach in the autumn and chub and grayling in the winter; and every now and then we would be interrupted by the explosive power of a salmon, pike or barbel.

All this within a short stroll from the back door.

Our utopia wouldn't be complete without a path winding down the valley to a cliff top, where it zig-zags down to the sea. The bass and mullet here would provide pleasant contrast to our freshwater fun and the sea and sand a playground for any off-spring and significant other with whom we share our world.

Admittedly this imaginary piece of landscape could only ever exist in our minds, but what a place to escape to. All the fishing we could ever wish for within a gentle walk of our home. It would be perfect . . . wouldn't it?

Perhaps not.

In his 1989 novel *A History of the World in 10½ Chapters*, Julian Barnes explores a heaven projected directly from our dreams. His protagonist swiftly comes to terms with his 'death' as he immerses himself into a perfect existence; mixing with dead heroes and enjoying as much sex and golf as he can cope with.

Before long his golf handicap is tumbling and his ability growing. With money no barrier, he buys the most up to date equipment and just gets better and better until finally he shoots the perfect round.

Eighteen holes in one. A round impossible to better, and suddenly the actual reality of a 'perfect' existence became apparent. What next? Shooting round after round of holes-in-one is simply banal. There is no challenge. No worth. Eventually he follows the path of all before him and chooses to 'die' a second time, only this time the end is final.

I am not suggesting for a second that angling, with its infinite anomalies and complexities should be considered on an equal footing to golf, but there is a warning to be learned in Barnes' words.

One of the reasons we love to fish is to escape. To detach ourselves from the day to day drudge of a nine to five and to lose ourselves in a world where time and pressures are, temporarily at least, suspended.

If my fishing paradise were to exist beyond my dreams, would I revel in it? I would stumble out of the door and be fishing for whatever I wished, but as nice as it may seem, I don't think my enjoyment would last much beyond a single season. In fact, I know it wouldn't.

Last year my wife and I moved west to Dorset. We found a cosy little cottage and though the nearest river is just a few miles distant and the sea within sight only if we climb the hill behind the house, we do have a lake tucked between the trees in the valley beside us, just a two minute walk away.

Naturally, I fished it the very evening that we moved in and for the next month I cast almost every day.

The lake is small, perhaps an acre, and holds a fair head of carp that though not true 'wildies' are directly descended from fish stocked by twelfth century monks into the waters of Glastonbury Abbey.

They do not grow large, but fight like fury and can give exciting sport on balanced tackle.

I only fish for them on the surface, with chunks of breadcrust on the simplest rig of all - a hook tied direct to the mainline and nothing else.

They can feed confidently especially if the bait is tight into the lily pads, but the lake is also home to a profusion of small roach which can batter a bait to nothing in a matter of seconds. I didn't mind them at first and played the percentage game. Every now and again a far bigger mouth would nudge the small fry out of the way and I would bend into a carp. I fished short sessions of an hour or so, picking off carp regularly and occasionally taking three or four in quick succession. The fishing culminated in the capture of a 14-pounder. A stunning lean fish which dived repeatedly for the sanctuary of the lily-pads before rolling into the net.

The roach however, were beginning to drive me mad and I

tired of the constant rebaiting and recasting. I began to cast only at fish I could see, which was fine on warm sunny evenings, but on a shallow, spring-fed lake the weather doesn't need to change much for the fish to simply disappear, and I would often creep a full circuit of the bank without so much as baiting a hook.

By mid-autumn I had stopped casting altogether and though I still visited the lake daily, mainly in order to collect firewood, I felt no urge to fish.

It felt odd, but all the while I knew I could go whenever I pleased, and that was enough. I didn't go just for the sake of fishing, and the less I fished, the more my time was consumed in other activities. I was writing a novel and foraging mushrooms, fishing became low priority.

Having angling opportunity on my doorstep actually meant I was fishing less than I ever had and towards the end of the season I understood why.

Tales of prowling perch were filtering through from the upper reaches of the river Kennet where I had spent much of the previous half dozen winters chasing stripes. I had enjoyed some lovely fishing on the clear upper reaches and would often not see another angler. It was over a hundred miles to the river now, but my friend Chris lives almost exactly half way and was as keen as me to go and chase his favourite winter quarry.

I even persuaded him to make an early start, arriving at his house at six o'clock, and this is a man renowned for his dislike of rising before noon.

The afternoon before the trip I borrowed a garden fork and turned over a damp corner of the garden. It was alive with worms, and I soon collected a hundred. The process and effort of collecting bait began to invoke a deep excitement. I washed my hands and readied my tackle. Picking out a couple of favourite floats and popping them in the pocket of my coat, along with a few shot, float rubbers, hooks and forceps. That would be all I would need. The river was narrow and clear where we were headed and best suited to a light and mobile approach. There was a reasonable head of perch, but they were wily and well scattered and swims that held fish one week could be completely empty the next. I did slip a pair of scales into my coat as well, though - fishermen are ever optimistic.

That night I barely slept. After a period of mild stagnation, I was about to inject some much needed life into my season, and it was due to the power of anticipation.

I was wide awake at three and didn't waste too much time battling to get back to sleep. It was time for tea and a very early breakfast.

Chris' house was at least an hour away, but I gave myself a little longer in order to avoid the main road and point the car instead along the dark back lanes.

There are very few occasions when pre-dawn journeys are voluntary, let alone pleasurable. Past jobs have seen me rise with just a handful of hours of sleep in my eyes before settling behind the steering wheel - often with a couple of hundred miles before me. On other occasions I have joined the ranks of commuters on the railway platform, as they line up at the precise points where the train doors will open, some supping coffee from plastic cups, others with their noses in the business pages, but not one wearing a smile.

This morning, though, was one of those occasions when I was not bemoaning my lack of sleep, and nor was I hurrying.

I had all the time I needed to enjoy the drive and after a couple of miles began to realise the significance of the journey itself. It was a vital piece of the jigsaw. The excitement that had built through the previous hours was now manifesting as a state of being.

The local wildlife had reclaimed the road in the darkness. I stopped a couple of times for deer and once for a badger. Rabbits scattered in the headlights and my eyes were darting around in the hope of glimpsing a barn owl. I didn't see one, but did spot a tawny peering down from an overhanging bough. I was already settled into the rhythm of the day, and the expectant excitement of the previous hours merely heightened this feeling. My mind, though distracted by the wildlife, centred itself around the day ahead. I was looking forward to seeing the river again, and sharing it with Chris. We would probably have the place to ourselves and would creep the banks and run our floats through familiar pools. There would be changes though, subtle differences. The folded reed stem that had pointed to a perch hotspot last season would be gone, and the high water of late summer may have permanently removed the snag from my favourite swim in the world. That wouldn't matter though, the water would crease in new directions for us to follow.

My fishing soul had reawakened. I was feeling sharp but also slightly detached as my focus readjusted. With fishing on tap and on my doorstep I had lost my way, but now, as the car trundled beside a twisting snake of catseyes, I was heading back to where I should be . . .

In 1802 William Wordsworth journeyed to France with his sister Dorothy, leaving London in the early morning of July

31st. It was to be an emotional trip as they were travelling to visit Wordsworth's former lover Annette Vallon and their daughter Caroline. Wordsworth had met Vallon in 1791, when, having travelled extensively through Europe, he found himself in France and fascinated by the Republican Movement.

Their romance was swift and passionate and they planned to marry, but a lack of money and growing tensions between his home and adopted countries forced Wordsworth to return to England in 1793, not long after Caroline's birth.

For the next eight years, Britain and France became embroiled within the French Revolutionary Wars, and Wordsworth was unable to make a return across the Channel until the Treaty of Amiens brought temporary respite in the spring of 1802. By now the sadness at the separation had been hardened by time, and though Wordsworth would certainly have travelled with great purpose for his daughter's sake, he was also in love with another woman, Mary Hutchinson, whom he intended to marry.

His mood would certainly have been reflective as he left London that morning, and perhaps that helped open his eyes a little wider as the coach crossed Westminster Bridge.

London was still quiet at such an early hour, and the smoke-less air (to which he later referred) brought a view of the city that belied the pollution that normally blackened the sky and poisoned the Thames below.

'Composed Upon Westminster Bridge' is one of Wordsworth's most celebrated sonnets, and was inspired wholly by the images of that morning, with the Thames at its heart. Wordsworth suggests that the river 'glideth at his own sweet will', a personification that is as evocative as it may have seemed unlikely.

Though Wordsworth was not famed for his skill as a fisherman, his words have inspired anglers since. One of whom, Lord Edward Grey, seemed so affected that his fishing trips would always begin with a nod to Wordsworth, as he crossed the Thames and viewed so differently London's life-blood.

Grey stood as Foreign Secretary from 1905 to 1916 - longer than any other figure in that office. He was also Ambassador to the US, leader of the Liberal Party in the House of Lords and Chancellor of Oxford University, but surely his finest accolade came as author of the 1899 book, *Fly Fishing*.

Grey schooled in Winchester, alongside the trout rich water of the river Itchen, and wrote fondly of his first forays into fishing. His initial attempts were crude and his only capture was 'a tiny thing, hopelessly under the limit of size for the Itchen'.

The river was fished by some of the more eminent anglers of the day however, men like Francis Francis and George Selwyn Marryat. Grey watched these great Victorians plying their art and learnt the intricacies of casting for chalkstream trout. He caught his first 'proper' fish, a pounder, on a red quill gnat, and the Itchen remained close to his heart for the rest of his fishing life.

In later years, when Grey was living in London, he would take the train from Waterloo to Winchester in order to fish his favourite waters and it was then that the words of Wordsworth seemed to influence his idyll. Grey urges the angler not to take a hansom cab to make his way to the station, but to enjoy the early morning on foot.

The best plan, however, is to live within a walk of Waterloo, and as you cross the river in the early summer morning, you may feel more reconciled to London than at any other time, and understand Wordsworth's tribute to the sight from Westminster Bridge.

To Grey, his engagement within the actual journey to the river seems to have been as important as any other aspect of the day. Living in Victorian London would only have accentuated this belief, as the contrast between the lead heavy smog of the Capital and the sweet fragrance of a chalkstream valley would have been extraordinary. But also, like Wordsworth, Grey urges the Londoner to embrace his city at an early hour when it is still snoozing in the half light. In that way the angler is conditioning his mind for the day ahead.

As I slowed into the quiet lanes of south Wiltshire, and into the drive of Chris' house, my thoughts were certainly not filled with romantic poetry. I was thinking of nothing but perch, and the sight of a float dibbing and burying as I inched it along the edge of the reeds.

Remarkably, Chris was not only awake, but dressed and ready to go. He opened the door as I reached to knock but before either of us spoke an unexpected but familiar sound broke into the silent morning.

A blackbird - the first of the year. His voice was rusty and his song somewhat shorter than it would be in a few weeks, but nevertheless it was enough for Chris and I to beam widely at one another. The first fingers of dawn were stretching up from the east, Chris had already finished his vital early morning cup of tea, and we were on our way before the engine of my car had stopped ticking.

I knew the first part of the second leg of my journey, but once we had rattled through the empty roads of Salisbury, Chris manoeuvred the car on to roads I had not before travelled.

I don't travel well as a passenger in a car. Motion sickness can be tortuous, especially on unfamiliar roads where I cannot counter the sway of each bend or twisted camber. But it was not a concern this morning. Chris is a sound driver, but more of a tonic was the flood of conversation between us. We were both sleep starved due to excitement, and that kind of condition, which is probably unique to angling, actually increases your focus rather than depletes it. Also, and we couldn't help but come back to this point, though the river would be painfully low we knew where the fish would be hiding. We had past experience, but more importantly we had also had a tip-off from our friend Martin.

Martin does not drive which is something of an inconvenience to a lover of the countryside living in south London. He had made the trek via public transport to this little stretch of the Kennet just five days before us.

His initial report had been disappointing. The river was desperately low with little weed growth. Two or three of the swims where we had consistently taken fish the previous winter had all but vanished. He had found a pocket of cover just above a sharp bend though, and though it was a pool with little previous form, decided it was a good place to make the first cast of the day. Martin ended up making his final cast of the day in the same hole, having found the perch stacked up under a small undercut of weed. With fish to 2lb 13oz, his long journey home was made with a contented glow.

Chris and I discussed where we would start our day and agreed that we would leave Martin's swim until later in the afternoon. Naturally, though, we both knew that that was exactly where we would be heading first.

The train is a method of transport I have never used in order to go fishing. Well, not properly at least. When I was in my teens I used to regularly holiday with my friend Leigh and his dad and two uncles in Ireland. We all fished, with varying degrees of success, and always had fantastic fun.

Work took Leigh's family to the Midlands, though, and one year, before I could drive, I had to take the train.

The journey there was fine. I was buoyed by the trip ahead, but the return leg was horrendous. Our final day on the river-bank was spent in classic Irish weather, and the rain did not stop throughout the journey home. Back at Birmingham International, I peeled my fishing gear from the roof rack and shoved it on to the train.

The only place I could fit all my kit was in the door space at the end of the carriage, which was fine until a large puddle of water began to form around me. My rod bag was absolutely saturated and was rapidly depositing water across the floor. By the time the train reached Leamington the water stretched the width of the carriage and I averted my eyes as people getting on the train had to step uneasily through a rising lake.

The guard came through and shook his head, snatching my ticket with a look of thunder and grumbling throughout. I shrank smaller and smaller but didn't know what to offer in the way of solution. I was also becoming ever more aware of the smell.

The weather in southern England seemed to be a trifle warmer than it had been in Ireland, and my wet fishing gear began to gently cook. Fortunately it was one of the proper old fashioned trains which had operable windows, so I slid each one down as far as they would go. It helped, sort of, but also succeeded in wafting the whiff further down into the carriage. There were audible groans and glances of displeasure shot in my direction. I could do nothing but stare at my feet, and that was when I noticed the maggots.

Presumably one or both of my parents collected me from the station and took me home, but I have little further memory of that journey. Sometimes, when events reach an uncontrollable nadir, the mind seems to shut down and block out the world in a defiant act of self-preservation. My final, conscious thoughts on that train ride were at least rational, however. Maggots weren't cheap, and I could not let any more escape - I would be able to use them on my next trip when I would almost certainly have been on my bike.

Every fisherboy should have a pond within cycling distance, and I was fortunate to have one at the perfect distance.

Alresford Pond was the venue where I cut my angling teeth. It was a tough, natural lake, heavily silted in the most part but with the occasional deep hole amid the clear water fed by a chalkstream tributary of Lord Grey's favourite river Itchen. It was a little over four miles from my childhood home, just far enough to stop me from spending my whole life there, but reachable in twenty minutes if the tench were likely to be feeding.

The route was effectively one long drag over Abbotstone Down: a large roll of chalkland which was once the site for one of Oliver Cromwell's many batteries and latterly a designated launch pad of nuclear warheads during the Cold War.

For a teenage cyclist it meant a steady mile and a half incline followed by a similar distance of freewheeling, which when driven by the excitement of fishing, made for the ideal pre-angle.

I would pump hard up the long hill, rod strapped to the frame, rucksack on my back, and find my legs so energised with the prospect of the water that I barely broke sweat. The glide down the other side would be a pacey but serene flight through downland, forest and cornfields. I would nudge forty mph at the steepest part, and once even overtook a car (an Austin Allegro) which was pretty much the coolest thing I had achieved at that point in my life.

The final half mile or so to the pond was mostly flat, but a double bend brought the road up alongside a church and normally the first whiff of water. Alresford Pond did not smell especially pleasant. In fact, on a summer evening when the water level was low it was pretty rank. The exposed silt would steam through the day and the stagnant odour would fall back earthwards as the sun began to set. A faint musk on the breeze though, was perfectly simulating. It meant I was nearly there. It was time to try and influence my luck. If I could weave both tyres round the next catseye without touching either white line then I would catch a tench. Then double or quits for a brace - or a guarantee that the 'roach pool' would be free.

It often worked.

As dawn dissolved into daylight so the traffic increased, but Chris and I were making steady progress. We had skirted the western end of Salisbury Plain and had snuck off down a side-lane which was going to save us at least fifteen minutes. I was surprised at Chris' knowledge of the area, but shouldn't have been. Twenty years ago he had trodden this route regularly while involved in the filming of a television series, one episode of which was set on the Kennet not far from where we were headed.

It was with slightly mixed feelings that Chris reminisced about the experience. There were many good days to recall from the project and a legacy that has grown with time, but there were also long hours spent away from his young family and the pressures of translating his love for fishing on to celluloid.

Of course, capturing the essence of angling on film was never going to be achieved without seriously hard graft, and when the light is just right the camera needs to roll. For Chris, the tough schedule and early morning calls were draining, but then he is a soul who has always struggled to contain himself within the structures of organised society. He is a man who has never suppressed his inner child, and the outlook and attitude that have developed as a result could not be any more inspiring.

The beauty of angling memories, of course, is that the angling itself will always lodge positive images into the mind. Any negativity is soon swept downstream with a red-tipped float offering infinite possibility in its stead. Water, and in particular running water, is ever changing, ever evolving, and just the thought of it can be sufficient to sweep through our recollections to leave a happy stream of moments glistening in the sun.

A red kite grabbed our attention, lolloping in the half light over a ploughed field to our left. It would not have been airborne long and was a welcome reminder of both our position geographically and within Man's tolerance of such beautiful birds.

We were in kite country now; the descendants of birds introduced into the Chiltern Hills a couple of decades ago had pushed south and west and were thriving.

My four-year old nephew Bertie, who lives in Pewsey a dozen miles or so to our west, could identify a kite from a buzzard before he reached eighteen months, and has seen so many that he barely raises an eye to one now. It is amazing to consider that when I was his age, there would have been less than fifty pairs in the whole of Britain. Thanks to the reintroductions and the massive efforts to maintain the native Welsh population there are nearer 3000 pairs today, ten per cent of the world population.

Chris and I would enjoy the company of the kites today; two pairs nest within a cast of where we would be fishing, and they are particularly 'user-friendly' raptors, happy to come close to people, a habit that we appreciate now, but one that aided their demise amid the heavy persecution of past centuries.

Red kites have yet to spread as far as my home in west Dorset, but are a familiar sight to Chris. They have bred in his valley for two or three years now, and this season have begun to show at his favourite crucian pond. The pond is only a fifteen minute drive from Chris' home, a lovely delving route through a warren of narrow wooded lanes and secret greensand cottages. A little over halfway is a gateway where Chris always stops the car in order to lean on the gate and admire the view, an action that is deeper than simple ritual.

The first time I joined Chris to fish the crucian ponds, he talked excitedly of the view as we approached the gateway. I was curious, but also dogged by a level of impatience. I spent my working week in a stress filled office at the time and as a result was overly distracted by a need to catch fish. Such impatience is counterproductive. If you are in a rush to simply get there, then this translates into your angling. You will be noisy, clumsy, will cast too fast, and if by some fluke you get a bite, the strike will be far too jerky and aggressive and the chance will be gone. Of course, when you are caught up in a world of impossible deadlines or share your desk with a telephone that never stops ringing, it is hard to simply switch off your mind from such conditioning. Certainly I, as Chris pulled up at the gate to show me *the view* for the first time, felt slightly torn.

'It looks lovely, but let's get fishing!' the over-eager part of my mind was whispering, 'Wait! No! What's he doing? Don't get out the car . . .'

But I am so glad he did.

I leant on the gate next to Chris and breathed. Breathed properly. Long and deep.

It was an incredible view. The wild meadow by our feet folded over into a small crease of woodland hiding, presumably, a water course that fed the sprinkle of houses down to our right. A square church tower was the only building to fully break the leafy cover and its form was softened slightly by the haze of warm air.

Beyond the valley to our left bulged a grassy hill whose head was capped in a deep green of mixed woodland. A single cottage sat on the edge of the trees, looking snug with its back sheltered against any cold northerly winds and the front kissed warm by the afternoon sun.

The most striking sight though, was the recurring wooded ridges that led to the horizon from our right. A giant must have laid his hand there too long and let each finger became blanketed by a thousand trees, a splay of digits pointing north but offering such stature in symmetry that your eye refused to follow their allusion.

Chris suggested that we could be looking at a grand Corsican panorama. I suddenly realised that the day had actually only just begun.

I would guess it was around eight o'clock when Chris and I pulled up alongside the Kennet. There was plenty of mist hanging across the water meadows, but we felt no rush to leap out and put up the rods.

Such was our anticipation, our nurtured excitement, that to actually now be here, in the place where we could fill the gaps with reality and make our hopes tangible, was slightly terrifying.

Within actuality come the countless idiosyncrasies that angling always throws at us, but that is the very reason why we love to fish.

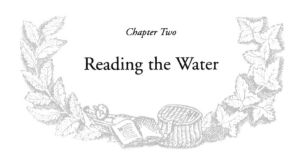

Chapter Two

Reading the Water

A river seems a magic thing. A magic, moving, living part of the very earth itself.
LAURA GILPIN

It was a tough decision for a novice cyclist, which hill to tackle first?

Northington Hill was steeper, but shorter as a result, an intense quarter mile of stand-up cycling, strangely eased by a tunnel of trees which seemed to suck you along.

The long open sweep of Kite's Hill was kinder for a time, but seemed never-ending to an eight-year-old, and the lack of cover made it more difficult to get off and push. Somebody might be watching.

Ultimately though, the decision was always made in favour of Kite's Hill, and it had nothing to do with the gradient. The triangular route twice crossed the Candover Stream, a winterbourne that meets the Itchen below Alresford, and the real reason for the bike ride was the chance to lean over the railings and gawp at the water below.

Kite's Hill was upstream of Northington, and therefore presented less flow and less chance of spying a fish - an awful lot can change in half a mile of winterbourne.

Though small brown trout would often push up the stream, the most common fish was the bullhead and any small stream adventurer will know that the best way to see a bullhead is to get in the water and turn over stones. Family holidays often found us near small streams and my brother Richard and I would spend hours flipping stones and chasing shadows. Curiously however, I never dipped my feet in the Candover Stream. There was an element of risk to it, not in the sense of physical danger, but rather that every pair of eyes in the valley would either know my name or at the least know who my family were. My parents would not have minded me fooling about in the water, but the valley contained more than its fair share of head-shakers and tut-tutters who would take pleasure in whispering between themselves about the Parr boy who plays where he oughtn't.

A stronger reason for my dry feet was the water itself. Not that it was wet, but that long before I was aware of the life within it, I was captivated by its very being.

Any small child crossing a waterway *has* to take a look, not because they are looking for fish or birds but because here is a world so different to their own. Water comes from taps and clouds, and yet here is something altogether different. This water is alive. It turns and creases and bubbles and slows. It carries colour and vibrance and moves of its own free will.

To consider that this living thing has a beginning or end is simply too great a thought for a young mind. All that matters is the right here, right now.

Of course, the next time that this child crosses the same bridge, they have to look again, they need reassurance that the course still exists. And while it invariably does, it will seem different to the image in their minds. It might be deeper, dirtier, angrier, or it might have relaxed and receded, sparkling like a quartz cascade.

Regardless of its state it remains a fascination, and as my childhood self abandoned his bike to the bushes and checked for a lack of oncoming cars or tractors, it was the anticipation of the water that grabbed him.

What would I see today? How would it feel?

A sedge stem might nod against the current, or the tiniest of eddies spiral off from the flow. 'Whirlpool!' my mind would shout. Pond skaters were favourites, dimpling the surface with curled feet. I had more trust in the creatures that lived on the dry side of the veil. Water boatmen would make me shudder, and I would urge the skaters to keep out of their way.

In the woodyard adjacent to our garden stood a disused dumper truck, whose shovel was always full of rainwater. I would always dare myself to peek in and would always recoil in revulsion.

The water itself would be algaed and part-stagnant, but it was the water boatmen that carried the greatest menace. These were the biggest boatmen in the world and they would paddle up from the darkness and sit coldly beneath the surface. I could never work out how they got there, but perhaps it was better that I didn't know they could fly.

As the years passed and the little pumping station in the valley bored deeper into the chalk, so the stream became ever more the winterbourne. Small pockets of water remained, but insufficient amounts to sustain the life once present. Some of the older locals reminisced of the great minnow migration, the stream blackening every spring as thousands pushed their way toward the headwaters. Two miles upstream was an acre or two of boggy scrub which had once been a shallow lake teeming with eels. One chap spoke of their abundance. He would set lines at night and never fail to catch. Eel pie was a staple part of his diet.

Sadly, the demise of the stream has been echoed by the decline of the eel. A fish that once filled every waterway has vanished altogether from many. The problem with an animal so prolific is that they can disappear almost unnoticed, and because they are taken largely for granted, we actually know very little about them. Certainly the eel, breeding as it does on the other side of the Atlantic, is a case in point. So much of their breeding and life cycles has been based upon conjecture, that now the future survival of the species is possibly dependant on Man's interference; it might be too late to help.

I never saw an eel in the Candover, though I have no doubt they were there. Lurking in the dark water of an undercut bank, or tucked up in the darkness beneath one of the bridges.

I had mixed feelings about eels. Their serpentine appearance left me a little wary, and tales from my father of their giant cousins, conger eels, made me shudder at the thought of dipping a toe anywhere I couldn't see the bottom - and not just in the sea.

My Dad had once caught a conger on a long line that was over six feet long. To a child, anything that was longer than my father was tall had to be respected.

Scarier still was the tale my dad told of diving off the rocks off Seacombe in south Dorset. One day he came face to face with a conger whose head was far bigger than his own, and they had a few moments of tense stand off before my father made a hasty retreat.

He is fairly unflappable, my father, but when he told that tale there was a tone of fear in his voice.

If I had any doubt of the mysterious nature of eels, I was left with none after a family holiday in Snowdonia.

In what was unusually warm and sunny weather for North Wales, we had followed a small stream upriver and found a lovely deep pool beneath a small stone bridge. There was ample water for us kids to dive and swim, while our parents readied a picnic on the bank.

We stayed all afternoon, splashing around until the air began to cool as the sun dipped below the mountains. As we dried ourselves, my brother noticed a movement.

"Eel!" he shouted, but the glimpse was fleeting.

As we gathered and stared, however, the boulder strewn stream-bed began to move. There were eels everywhere.

I was fascinated. Torn between the sight of so many big fish in such a small stream, and the unease of knowing just how close my toes had been to them.

We watched them until the light faded and the surface glassed over in the twilight. The eels were no doubt moving up and down stream to feed, venturing into the shallower glides and riffles under cover of darkness. It may seem an obvious lesson now, but the experience helped me to understand the nature of fish.

The deep, slow pool had offered perfect sanctuary for the resting eels. They could snooze beneath the boulders out of sight and safe in number, and untroubled by strong currents. There wouldn't be sufficient food in this one pool for such a number of fish, but as nocturnal feeders they could disperse to the more oxygenated, weed filled runs where invertebrates would be plentiful, filling their stomachs and heading back to the pool before dawn.

My young mind had not really considered fish behaviour before this moment. Nor how the subtleties of change within the water could dictate a fish's actions. I had thought that fish lived in very particular places; that they would be spaced evenly along any given stretch of water.

So it was that I began looking differently at the Candover stream.

Though its flow diminished each year, my increasing age meant that I was pedalling ever further away from home.

A cycle ride to meet friends in Alresford could be made via the hamlet of Abbotstone, where the stream flowed with more purpose and the herons would hunt with more optimism. The stone bridge from which I would gaze always had a trout or two below it - and they were good sized fish, occasionally nudging a pound in weight.

I began to learn exactly where the fish would be lying, and more importantly the reasons why.

The safety provided by the bridge itself was fairly obvious. Hidden from the eyes of non aquatic predators, the trout could lie under the darkness of the stonework without spooking from every shadow. But the flow itself was a hindrance; being funnelled through a man-made structure, the water would bubble and churn making it impossible to hold station in the current without expending exhaustive amounts of energy.

Far better was the slack immediately below the bridge's central stanchion. The water here was well oxygenated but also easy on the fins and should danger present itself, then the dark water beneath the bridge itself was just a tail flick away.

Moreover any items of food being swept along the main flow would pass right in front of the trout's nose. A swift dart into the current and a steady food source could be tapped with minimal effort.

There would usually be two or three fish sharing the slack, often almost touching one another. The biggest fish always lay with his nose closest to the main flow, and would muscle his way back into prime position each time he left it to grab a passing insect. I would frequently lose track of time watching these fish, though it was hard not to spook them. I would have to inch my forehead over the edge of the stonework until they came into view, and thereafter stay absolutely still. The slightest movement would cause panic.

Around twenty yards above the bridge was a shallow ridge in the centre of the stream, immediately below a shallow bend. The slightly deeper water just behind the ridge was another favourite trout lie, though a fish in residence there would have to station itself slightly across the flow in order to intercept any passing food. The main current would push hard against the ridge itself before sliding downstream. By watching leaves in the flow (and presuming food items would be affected in the same manner) I could see how turbulent the water alongside the ridge actually was. A leaf would be twirled in a rapid corkscrew before being spat out at pace, and would be past the nose of the trout in a moment. The stream riffled across very shallow water just below this spot, so any fly missed could not then be chased downstream. Instead the fish would have to dart out, make a grab, and then continue hard across the current before making its way back to its initial position.

There seemed to be an awful lot of hard work involved, but

it was clearly worth the effort - there was always a fish in that spot and always one of the biggest trout in the stream.

Like many children, I absorbed myself in the world of *Swallows and Amazons*.

Arthur Ransome used various locations for his tales, but my favourites were definitely those based among the lakes and mountains of Cumbria.

I loved the adventure and the imagery, the references to birds of prey (especially the peregrines), and, of course, the fact that Ransome had such a passion for life within the water and not just upon it.

In *The Picts and the Martyrs*, a surprise and unwelcome visit by Nancy and Peggy's Great Aunt scuppered the planned visit of Dick and Dorothea, who instead made refuge in an abandoned shepherds cottage in the woods.

They are forced to live off the land (with supplements from the Amazons' kitchen) and meet a local lad called Jacky who teaches them to tickle trout.

When they encounter Jacky he is lying on his stomach clinging to a tree with one hand and working the water with the other. After just a few seconds he scrambles to his feet with a small trout. Jacky encourages Dorothea to have a try, and points her to a spot beneath the near bank where he knows a fish will be lying. Dorothea is hesitant, but Jacky clearly knows the river intimately and also the habits of trout.

'Catch yin today and there'll be another in t'same spot in t'morning.'

He may be a fictional character with a stereotypical turn of phrase, but Jacky's observations are still true today, as I discovered on my local stream.

Though I never attempted to tickle them, I would know exactly where fish would be lying day after day. As I began to explore further afield, to the rivers Itchen and Arle, so the pattern was mirrored. These rivers also held stocks of grayling and pike which behaved in the same manner as the trout - favouring particular lies which offered them safety and food with maximum efficiency.

One fish in particular caught my eye in the river Arle - a pike of around fifteen pounds that used to sit in the same position every time I walked the river.

There was a slight depression in the riverbed where she could lie still with the current passing over her head. Water crowfoot grew thick around her lair and if it wasn't for a very handily placed alder tree, I might never have noticed her.

I spent many school lunch-breaks up that tree - watching and waiting. Not once, though, did she even seem remotely interested in making a grab for anything.

What was especially fascinating was the presence of her courtiers. Not pike, but trout, all around the pound mark and always sitting either side of her tail.

They reminded me of the pilot fish that would cluster around sharks on the wildlife films on television, keeping the shark free from parasites while enjoying the protection that came from swimming with one of the most feared predators of the sea.

It is a relationship that has forever fascinated naturalists and writers.

About the Shark, phlegmatical one,
Pale sot of the Maldive sea,
The sleek little pilot-fish, azure and slim,

How alert in attendance be.
From his saw-pit of mouth, from his charnel of maw
They have nothing of harm to dread,
But liquidly glide on his ghastly flank
Or before his Gorgonian head:
Or lurk in the port of serrated teeth
In white triple tiers of glittering gates,
And there find a haven when peril's abroad,
An asylum in jaws of the Fates!
They are friends; and friendly they guide him to prey,
Yet never partake of the treat-
Eyes and brains to the dotard lethargic and dull,
Pale ravener of horrible meat.

The Maldive Shark by Herman Melville (1888)

Melville may be more familiar for his tale of a great white whale, but his observations of pilot fish and their symbiotic relationship with sharks demonstrate a depth of appreciation of the natural world that ran far deeper than was typical in the nineteenth century.

Moby Dick himself was ultimately portrayed as a whale not motivated to hunt humans, but instead an enigma whose sheer size and power could sink ships should he need to defend himself.

The pike in the Arle, my own Moby Dick, seemed similarly disposed, to the extent that she did not actually appear to hunt anything.

I wondered if the trout drew lots, and sacrificed themselves in return for the protection she gave them from all the feisty jacks in the river. Certainly they would not be keeping her free from parasites as the pilot fish would. Trout are not the most complex of fish, and though flighty through instinct, do not appear to learn as other species, such as carp, do.

Perhaps that is due to the fact that they only get to make one single mistake before finding themselves in the bottom of an angler's creel, whereas a carp may be hooked dozens of times within its life.

I rather felt that these fish had broken the mould and were learning. They knew that safety came from lying with the queen of the stream, and they could pick flies off the surface (as I watched them do) without her even flicking a pectoral. They had incorporated instinct into their learnings though, and when they felt that mild electrical bolt as the pike stirred from her torpor and her lateral line crackled in response to hunger, they would sink back and either flee or bury themselves into the weed until food had been found and the pike lay still once more.

An awful lot of thought went through my mind as I sat up that tree on my lunch breaks. I had my own fears to consider, too - the threat of being late for afternoon registration, and the fear of my mother's reaction should I stain my blazer on the bark of the bough,

It was a sad day when I climbed the tree and the pike wasn't there. I knew immediately that she must be dead; never had I seen her away from that spot and there was no reason to believe that her ritual had changed.

Lunchtimes were never the same, though curiously a small shoal of perch subsequently settled in the pike lair. I don't doubt that another big pike would have muscled them out in time, but I hadn't seen a fish in the river that was anywhere close to becoming the new matriarch.

A year or two later I met the chap who had caught and killed my queen. He was pretty damned blasé about it too. The river keeper gave him free fly fishing in return for his controlling of the pike stocks. The big fish had become something of a challenge to him; no matter what lure he had put past her nose, she had not once flickered.

Eventually he put a diving plug on his line and drew it hard and fast across her back, driving a treble hook into her flesh and then dragging her thrashing from the river where she was clonked on the head.

He was rather proud of his achievement, which spoke volumes about the man, and I am happy to say our paths have not crossed since. The pike had the last laugh, too. With no monster to keep them in check, the population of smaller fish exploded, filling the stream with a full squadron of jacks and jills who were soon big enough to start tucking into the trout stock.

I like to think that the 'fisherman' was subsequently relieved of his pike-snaring responsibilities and never got to cast a fly on the river again.

Though I grew up in the chalkstream heaven that is Hampshire, my own angling interests were channelled in a distinctly more coarse direction.

My father certainly influenced this, if only because he had a selection of old coarse gear tucked into a corner of the garage. His own involvement had fallen victim to the commitments of work, fatherhood and a garden full of vegetables, but as my brother and I took an interest, so he helped develop it.

The rodbag became a regular part of the holiday luggage, and narrow-boat holidays offered ample opportunity to drop a float into the water. Having spent so much time staring from bridges into crystal clear streams, the waters on which I was fishing were coloured and mysterious. A factor I rather liked.

The unknown always gave me hope, and if I was unable to see that there were no fish, then I could imagine that there were plenty.

Children are easily dispirited, and the unfailing optimism that my mind could create from a coloured pond became so embedded that I would see possibility in puddles on the road.

My understanding of clear streams certainly helped me to find fish in the ponds and canals, though. I knew fish liked cover, be it a weed-bed or overhanging tree, and I knew that they liked a bit of water over their heads. On a very base level, I knew that if I couldn't see them, then they probably couldn't see me, and would therefore behave as if I wasn't there.

Wind direction is a key factor on still waters. Anglers ever talk of 'fish following the wind' and there is plenty of sense behind this. Insects and items of food will be blown into specific areas where they are easy to find and eat. Similarly a warm breeze would lift the temperature of the upper water layers - perhaps only fractionally, but significant when you are cold blooded.

I may not initially have been aware that I was following the wind, but was drawn to those corners of water where the scum and surface detritus had formed a nice raft for fish to hide beneath.

These spots were generally easier to fish, too. Any tow on the water generated by the wind would be pushing into the very place where I wanted my float to sit, so there would be no need to repeatedly mend the line or recast.

With much of my early fishing years spent on stillwaters, when I found myself stirred by barbel around the age of twenty I had to learn how read a very different kind of water.

It was Martin, whom I met through mutual friends, that convinced me of the barbel's virtues. He had spent much of his fishing life chasing them on the river Kennet, and his tales certainly caught my interest.

We arranged a trip, and I suddenly realised just how inadequate I was. My river fishing experience was limited to trout caught on free-lined bread on the chalkstreams and a solitary but successful trip to the Mole in Surrey.

The stretch of the Kennet we first visited was quite unlike anything I had experienced.

A weir marked the top end, though the pool itself was inaccessible. The run-off was long, fast, shallow and weedy, a combination that frankly terrified me and I walked another hundred yards before seeing water I could comfortably consider casting into. Here, though, was a huge fallen tree that no doubt held fish, but also looked like angling suicide to cast towards.

A mill stream entered the river at this point, forming a wide, deep pool. I liked the look of the dark, quiet water, but where on earth would I put a bait?

Further on and the pool tailed off before funnelling through another series of rapids, and another hundred yards of water that looked beyond my abilities.

Eventually I settled in a fairly nondescript swim, a decision determined by the fact that I could just hold bottom with an ounce of lead (the biggest in my tackle box). I sat there biteless and clueless until dusk.

Though I felt totally out of my depth I also felt inspired by the challenge and we arranged a return trip for the following week.

This time, I travelled with less kit and spent much of the day simply walking the banks and watching the water. Every swim offered its own potential feature, from overhanging banks and bushes, to the steady runs between streamer weed and the slacks and big water of the weir pools.

Though the swim I eventually settled in was also comfortable to fish, the fact that I had considered it carefully beforehand, meant I was at least fishing with some confidence.

A few gudgeon fed, but nothing bigger, though this time I drove home with more faith than the previous week.

Another week passed and this time Martin suggested a different venue, The Old Mill at Aldermaston. It was a popular stretch but with good reason, being prolific for barbel.

We arrived early, far too early as it transpired. The gates didn't open for another two hours. We wandered down to the road bridge as the sun began to rise and peered down into the river below.

It was fairly shallow beneath the bridge but with thick beds of weed and a clean gravel bed. Within a minute or two, Martin was pointing.

"Barbel," he murmured, "and another."

I struggled to pick them out at first, but the scallop shaped pectoral fins gave them away, and once my eyes adjusted, I could see every detail.

They were not huge fish, maybe five or six pounds, but plenty big enough for my desires. They were the first barbel I had ever seen, and suddenly a fish that had felt uncatchable and almost unreal, was physically in front of me and wholly accessible.

As we watched, a steady stream of barbel moved upstream, all working from one clump of weed to another, and all seemingly heading for the deep, dark water that ran beneath the trees a hundred yards or so away.

Those were the spots we needed to fish, though we did not know the etiquette of the Old Mill at opening time. As the gates were opened, so the doors of the cars behind us (and there was quite a queue) were flung open and people literally ran to bag the prime swims. By the time Martin and I had gathered our tackle and thoughts together, the only free water was down towards the road bridge itself, where we had seen the fish vacate.

We had a chance, though; there might be a straggler, and I flicked a lump of luncheon-meat across to the tail of the deep run with expectation rather than hope.

The bite came immediately, and after a steady fight my first barbel was in the net. It was barely three pounds in weight, and had clearly had a recent run-in with a pike, but it was a fish I shall always cherish.

That was the only fish of the day, but we learned much from it. We spent far more time walking and looking than actually fishing, and having now made contact with a barbel, I felt more in touch with the river.

Martin explained the subtleties in the shape of the river's surface. The differences between the riffles created where the water ran shallow over gravel or the bulges displaced by a billow of crowfoot. Creases in the current where slow water met fast; the overhangs or rafts where chub would be lying, and the steady glides whose main feature was the smooth silky water itself.

Every subsequent trip to the Old Mill and elsewhere on the Kennet, began without any tackle in hand. I would roll a cigarette and walk the banks, tuning myself in to the rhythm of the water. The river would change from one day to the next, and success would come from recognising the slightest adjustment. It was not a case of thinking like a fish, more an unlocking of my own mind. An awareness that went beyond an understanding of the messages the river was showing me, to a part of my psyche that is one of the angler's most useful weapons. His sixth sense.

If your mind dances to the tune of the river, then so it presents an altogether different view of it. Occasionally, I simply know where and when to cast purely on instinct, and if I trust my hidden sense and respond to it, then I always find a fish.

An Idle Angler is not a lazy angler.

The lazy angler parks his car and plonks himself in the first available swim.

'The swims nearest the car-park are always good,' he will reason, and in some ways he is correct. Those spots will be fished more than any other and may well appear to be productive as a result. But what the lazy angler lacks is a control over time, or rather a refusal to respond to its constraints.

An Idle Angler will know that moments spent watching, breathing and absorbing are worth a thousand casts in the wrong place.

Sometimes it only takes one cast.

Chapter Three

Tackling Up

*To the man who only has a hammer, everything
he encounters begins to look like a nail.*
ABRAHAM MASLOW

We would often walk from my grandparents' house in Epsom across the green at the end of their road and into the woods beyond.

There the path slowly rose until it opened out to a mixture of scrub and heath where we once found an adder skin tangled in a gorse bush. We never saw a snake on the heath, but knowing they were there gave that part of the walk an extra edge. A mixture of intrigue and fear. I wanted to seem brave and unflustered, but I didn't stray too far from the path and carefully watched every step.

As we sloped down the other side of the hill, the first glimpse of water shimmered through the trees. It was the larger stew-pond, and the less exciting of the two. As we stood on the water's edge the lake felt cold and simply too vast. I could see the muddy bottom in the margins and I felt that if any fish lived here at all, then they would be far out in the middle where they could find enough water to cover their backs.

I didn't like the feel of this pond, as though it were too grown

43

up for me. The fact that I could stand so close to the water's edge created the sense of looking uphill, and that is a giddying sensation when looking at water.

In contrast, through the trees to the right was the smaller sister stew with an altogether different atmosphere. It was smaller and more compact, with a reed 'island' filling the centre and creating an intimacy that felt far more accessible than the bigger, colder top pond.

Tadpoles flicked around the margins where the water itself held sufficient colour to hide the bottom and surely fish.

One afternoon I noticed a length of baler twine tangled in a nearby bush and hatched an idea. I found a fairly lengthy stick and tied the twine to the end before flicking it on to the water's surface. Remarkably, and I remember my surprise, absolutely nothing happened. I had seen people fishing before and catching fish and I had the essential implements so why wasn't I catching?

"You need a hook and bait . . ." My grandfather whispered behind me, "and that line is probably a bit thick too . . ."

I was more confused than disappointed, and continued flicking the length of twine into the water. I had a cast at the tadpoles, too, but could see their lack of interest - perhaps my grandad was right.

I left my rod on the bankside, with the hope that someone else might have more success than I, and thought of fish for the whole walk back.

Once at my grandparents', my grandfather beckoned me down the garden to his shed. I had never ventured into the shed before, and in truth, had not really noticed it. To its right sat an Anderson Shelter, untouched since the Second World War and an awesome fascination for a young mind.

I would peek inside the darkness and imagine my family tucked up safe while German bombers whined overhead and bombs exploded all around. That such a shelter would not have proved impervious to the might of the Nazi airforce was inconceivable to my young mind, and proven by the fact that it still stood. Bombs would simply have bounced off the corrugated roof and rattled the door as they wrenched craters in the garden.

Suddenly though, I didn't care for the Shelter. Grandad had unlocked his shed and had a bag in his hand. A long, straight, brown cloth bag which he handed to me with a smile.

And there it was - my first fishing rod.

Whole cane, around ten feet long, with twists of wire as line guides and the odd knob and node that had proved too tough to sand.

It was far from straight, but I couldn't care a jot. It was mine.

In his 1912 work *Coarse Fishing*, H.T. Sheringham recommends that an angler needs three rods in order to cover the fundamental aspects of the art: a fly rod (to cover both coarse and game fish), a pike rod, and then the most important of the three - a 'general rod':

> *For the rod I counsel a weapon which will continue to have your affection and esteem after you have got out of the three rod stage, and have begun to realise that different fish and different rivers are best approached with different kinds of rod, or perhaps I should say, lengths of rod.*
>
> *Your first venture will not always meet your needs, but it should be of such a type that it will always meet some of your needs.*

My first rod met all of my needs until I fell into the common misconception that all of the fish lived in the middle of the pond.

I had christened it with roach and gudgeon on the Llangollen canal. Then stunted roach and rudd from a small pond nearer home. It even caught baby pollack and pout from various piers and jetties around the coast, and all the while it had performed quite adequately.

To get to the better fish in my local pond though, it seemed a longer cast was in order. I may well have weakened it by lifting out too many half-pounders in the days before I learnt what a landing-net was for, but ultimately it was my vicious casting action that snapped it in two.

My main concern at the time was that I wouldn't be able to carry on fishing, but it was a timely reminder, especially with Christmas close, that I needed a rod that could handle my pre-pubescent gusto.

An 11-foot fibreglass rod arrived on Christmas Day, and I was allowed to christen it that afternoon, breaking the ice and winkling out three tiny roach.

This was to be the rod to which Sheringham referred. It was classed as a 'match' rod, but was lumpy enough to handle the tench of Alresford Pond and even caught my first barbel.

A robust rod was perfect for my teenage self. It could survive being lashed to my bicycle frame and laid on gravel banks, and the solid through-action made it perfect for ripping tackle free from overhanging trees.

Most importantly, though, was the fact that I was becoming accustomed to having a fishing rod as an extension of my right arm.

A fly rod, with the reel at the butt, is designed to extend the wrist. It is light and easily managed in one hand, as its principal function is to repeatedly place the fly over a rising trout.

While the rod will need to handle any fish that is hooked, the action of casting is far more of an exertion for the rod and angler, and the caster needs to feel as if it is an appendage of his own body.

Chat to any fly fisherman on a chalkstream, and he will subconsciously use his rod as a tool of expression, pointing out fish and features as if it were a nine-foot index finger.

This is not a peculiarity but a basic human trait. As hunter-gatherers we would spend the vast proportion of our lives with a tool or weapon in hand, and in a time when life was so precarious, a mastery of apparatus could mean the difference between life and death.

For his role as Hawkeye in the 1992 film *Last of the Mohicans*, Daniel Day-Lewis recognised the importance of the character's relationship with his rifle. Day-Lewis is renowned for the lengths he will go to in order to master a role, and for this portrayal of James Fennimore Cooper's hero, he learned to live as Hawkeye would have in the mid-eighteenth century. He spent six months learning to live off the land; hunting, fishing, skinning animals for clothing - but as importantly he spent every second of his life with his rifle in hand.

The results are a credit to his dedication. In the film, Hawkeye's rifle is as much part of him as his arms or legs, to the extent that the gun does not appear as a weapon, but an extension of the character's personality.

While most fishermen are unlikely to have such a profound relationship with their favourite rod, such a familiarity is crucial to his success. And while the fly fisherman nurtures this rapport in order to master his cast, the coarse angler's most yielding consequence is during the fight itself.

The coarse rod is an extension of the forearm. The butt should nestle around the point of the elbow and rest comfortably beneath a straight wrist before the hand lightly grips the main point of balance around the reel fittings.

While holding the rod, the butt is levered into the arm, and should allow the angler to mend the line and tweak the float without feeling encumbered. When playing a fish, the wrist locks and any lunges are absorbed though the forearm and elbow, the joint of which levers with the rod.

While the choice of rod might be aesthetically pleasing, it does not catch the angler more fish. However, a rod that is familiar and rests in the hand with balance and a sense of belonging, will definitely land more fish.

The actual rod material is very much down to the angler's personal choice and wealth.

Carbon fibre is the most popular substance today, creating incredibly light and thin blanks.

Fibreglass is used very little having been superseded by carbon in the 1980s. It is more durable though, despite being heavier and bulkier, and will tend to stay in the rod bag for more years than a carbon equivalent.

A more traditional material is cane, sometimes whole (as was my first ever rod) but normally split.

Split-cane is considerably heavier than carbon or glass-fibre, but is far more responsive in the fight. Being a natural substance, the cane seems to absorb the lunges of a fish in a fluid manner, and hook pulls are less common as a result.

I personally have rods made from all three materials, and will use each depending upon the type of fishing I am doing. The two that I use most frequently and feel most comfortable using, are made from split-cane and fibreglass.

The split-cane rod is an Avocet, built just a decade or so ago as a through-action all purpose rod. It came to me via a piece of extreme generosity, and I christened it with a trip to a flooded river Kennet where a piece of luncheon-meat in a slack beneath my feet produced a barbel of over thirteen pounds.

I was a little undergunned to be honest, but I hadn't harboured any hope of hooking a fish that size. While the Avocet lacked the power to heave the fish away from the bottom, it did display a perfect action to counter the barbel's headshakes and dives. I knew within a minute that if I was patient I would land the fish, and so it proved. I ceded no line at all and just let the cane take the strain.

Since that barbel I have used the Avocet to catch chub, perch, crucians and tench. It is a little heavy for roach and a little stiff for dace and grayling, but having got to know its nuances, I feel confident using it in just about any situation.

The glass-fibre rod is a twelve foot Shakespeare 'coarse rod' and was probably made in the early to mid Seventies. Its action is similar to the Avocet though it is slightly softer and more suited to playing smaller, softer mouthed species.

Like my first ever rod, it was originally my grandfather's, and was spotted in a corner of his garage after his death. My uncle knew that I might have an interest in it and made sure it came my way.

It too was christened with a trip to the Kennet, though this time amid much more settled conditions. I coupled it up with

4lb breaking strain line to inch a float along a favourite run and hooked a chub first cast. The rod displayed far more power than I had expected and coped with the fish particularly well, and I netted a lovely, long chub of 5lb 10oz - the first and best of a nice bag that day.

While both rods have sentimental value, they both also satisfy Sheringham's criteria for a general rod. I have used both extensively and feel comfortable with either in my hand. Often, the only way I decide which I am going to take to the bankside is determined by whichever I first lay my hand upon.

Though carbon-fibre is by far the most common material in contemporary fishing rod production, even split-cane is a relatively modern component.

Bamboo was originally imported into Britain as a building material, and it was not until the mid nineteenth century that its qualities as a light and flexible tool with which to wield a fishing line was widely explored.

Previously, rods were fashioned from whole wood such as ash, and with reels, or 'winches', not becoming popular until the late eighteenth century, these rods would have been long and very heavy.

Izaak Walton, author of *The Compleat Angler* in 1653, makes no mention of the reel in the first edition of his celebrated work, though his contemporary Thomas Barker does make reference to a winch in his own book of 1651, *Barker's Delight*.

With no surviving models from this era, there is some conjecture as to whether the 'winch' was used in the same manner as anglers would use a reel today, or if it were simply a tool for line storage. Whatever the actuality, it appears likely that Walton himself used just a rod and line to create his own angle.

The line would have been made from horsehair, and Walton's great friend Charles Cotton describes how to form a tapered horsehair line in a later edition of *The Compleat Angler*. By beginning with two twisted strands and adding another strand to each length he formed a taper which would cast similarly to a modern day fly line. In some accounts anglers refer to the use of just a single hair, which led to epic battles such as that related by Francis Francis in his 1867 work *A Book on Angling* when he hooked a barbel.

It had long been dark, and he showed no symptoms of tiring, though he had in turn tired all of us. Playing a fish in the dark is awkward work, so we hailed some men, several of whom, attracted by the report of our having hooked 'a big 'un', were standing on the bank, to bring us a couple lanthorns and some hot brandy and water, for it was bitterly cold; and with the aid of the lanthorns we at length managed to get the net under the fish and lifted him out. It was half-past eight when he was landed, so that I had him on three and a half hours. And now what does the reader think he weighed? I was disgusted to find that he was only a six-and-a-half-pound fish; had I known it I would have broken from him hours before; but it turned out that he was hooked in the back fin, and his head being perfectly free, he of course played as heavily as fish of double the size; and even now, remembering what the stream was, I wonder how I did succeed in landing him, as a fish so hooked, having his broadside opposed to the water, has great powers of resistance. Indeed I consider that the accomplishment was equal to killing a fish of double the weight if fairly hooked.

Though this account is impressive enough in its telling, I was curious as to just how strong a single horsehair is. A fishing story is all the more impressive if an accurate perspective is placed upon it.

A neighbour keeps a horse and I asked her if she would procure me a handful of hair the next time he was groomed.

History suggests that horsehair was traditionally taken from the tail of a white horse before being dyed, whereas my hair came from jet-black tail of a Spanish stallion.

I would be very surprised if there is no variation of strength between different breeds of horse, but this is just one of the potential flaws in my rather un-scientific experiment.

I tied varying lengths of hair using various knots to my flyweight scales and gently pulled. Surprisingly, the hair rarely broke at the knot itself, and despite feeling rigid to the touch did offer a fair amount of stretch.

As I say, many a scientist would wince at my methods, but nevertheless I feel confident to state that a single horsehair from a Spanish Stallion breaks at, on average, 1lb and 4oz.

What is also clear from handling horsehair is that it has far less durability than modern day lines. Once stretched it narrows forming weak links, whereas good quality line today has no 'memory' - it returns to its original shape.

Further to my tests, it was interesting to note that the horsehair appears to have a similar diameter to the 4lb breaking strain line (made by Maxima) which I use for much of my fishing.

This is another reminder of just how fortunate the modern angler is.

For Francis Francis, the single horsehair was as fine a line as he could use, and yet it would appear clumsy and crude to many anglers today. Though barbel might not be fished for on 4lb line, many smaller species are targeted with lines far, far thinner. Of course, on the flipside, fish were less pressured in Francis' day and less suspicious as a result, and perhaps more importantly, they would generally be caught just once, ending up in a glass case or a cooking pot rather than back in the water with a wariness of fishing tackle.

The angler today has a bewildering choice of lines to use, but what is most important is that he builds a relationship with his line that is similar to that of his rods, and, indeed, the reels on which the line is kept.

If you are familiar with the nuances of your line, then it will only aid you when casting and playing a fish. You get to know just how much pressure you can apply and more importantly, the manner of that pressure. Some lines are braided or pre-stretched, giving a fine diameter for their strength but no 'give' during the fight. The rod should always balance against this rigidity and be soft enough to cushion the lunges of the fish.

The more familiar monofilament lines are fairly elastic, which is a quality useful for absorbing a fish's headshakes, but can make bites hard to hit at distance and can be pretty dangerous if the tackle gets snagged. An automatic response to the hook getting solidly embedded in a tree trunk is to pull for a break towards you. The line will stretch before snapping, propelling floats and weights at potentially lethal speed.

Despite this risk of injury, monofilament fills all of my spools, though this is as much down to cost as personal preference.

Some anglers will replace their line on a regular basis for fear of weakening due to weathering or wear, but I am far less fastidious. I will only replace it when there is no line left, and some of my reels have worn the same line for a decade or two. In all honesty, I do not recall ever having lost a fish due to line degradation, though I have certainly had breakages due to poor quality line. As with so many aspects of life, you get what you pay for, and the filthy-cheap bulk spools of shiny fishing line catch more anglers than fish. If you find a brand that you like and suits your style of fishing, then stick with it.

As for the tool on to which your line is winched, this too is ultimately down to personal choice.

The most commonly used reel is the fixed-spool. As its name suggests, the line sits on a static spool and is wound on via a rotating bale-arm which is operated by handle.

The bale-arm is flicked open when casting so that line leaves the spool unhindered and the design of the reel allows the incorporation of a gear system which enables a single turn of the handle to spin the bale-arm multiple times. This is particularly handy when fishing at long range as it speeds up the retrieve.

Fixed-spool reels normally use a drag system which essentially works as a clutch, tightening the spool itself so that under certain pressure it will turn and cede line. If used correctly, this can be of massive benefit when playing a large fish. If the fish makes a sudden run or dive then the reel will allow line to leave the spool before it snaps.

The centre-pin reel is more basic in appearance and function, being a single rotating drum. Its simplicity does not prevent it from having advantages over the fixed-spool, though.

When trotting a river, where a float is allowed to drift along in the current, the flow is often sufficient to turn the centre-pin and pull line at current pace. The thumb can be used to gently

brake the drum, holding back the float and encouraging the
bait to flutter up enticingly.

Another advantage when using a centre-pin is the direct contact made while playing a fish. The thumb or second hand can
be used to counter the rotation of the spool and allow the fish
line should it dive or run, whereas with a fixed-spool you have
to rely on backwinding or the clutch. This can make the fight
more intimate and enjoyable, though casting with a 'pin is
limited, and for distance fishing it is of no use.

The centre-pin looks similar to the reels used for fly fishing,
though the latter is used far more as a method of storage than
a tool of actual angling. Fly line is tapered (as Charles Cotton
described) so that when casting, the weight of the line is itself
sufficient to work the fly to the required lie, but deliver the tip-
pet gently on to the water.

In sea-fishing and freshwater lure fishing, a multiplier reel
may also be used. This also has a spool which is free-spinning
in order for casting a distance and also a gear mechanism in
order to speed the retrieve.

Whatever the reel, it should balance the rod, feel comfortable
in the hand and help you place your bait just where you want
it - and at every opportunity that bait should be fished beneath
a float.

In my angling infancy I was ridiculed for using a float. Such
is the power of fashion, even within a world so individual and
soulful as angling, that the *only* way to fish at the time was
ledgering.

The influence of modern carp fishing was filtering right down
to the small fry out for their first cast and the method itself was
an indication of proficiency.

The rod would always be placed on two rod rests pointing towards the ledgered bait.

The absolute beginner would then have a dough bobbin hanging on the line between the reel and first ring and acting as a bite indicator. This was only until he had pinched the top from the washing-up liquid bottle under the sink, which would hang freely on the line and display the angler's first right of passage.

In due course he would progress to monkey climbers, sliding bobbins on thin metal poles, before really mixing it with the big boys and purchasing bite alarms.

The ultimate goal was the 'rod-pod', a battery assembly of metal which incorporated both alarms and monkey climbers, and ensured that you would be taken seriously even if you didn't catch a thing.

And still I preferred using a float. I liked the way it sat pregnantly beside the lily pads and would signal the slightest fishy interest. And I definitely caught more fish through its sensitivity.

These fish, though, didn't really count. They were flukes. Even if I was catching finicky tench that were only twitching another angler's bobbins, somehow my catches were less virtuous because I wasn't ledgering.

Today I still use a float wherever and whenever possible, though circumstances will dictate the precise method. Sometimes, particularly on powerful rivers, the float is an inconvenience, and I certainly do not martyr my chances by using one when a ledgered bait will be more effective and efficient. In fact, when fishing for barbel or chub nothing is more exciting than touch-ledgering - feeling the line for a bite.

But if I have fished in such a way for too many trips then fixing a float on to the line brings a warm reminder of familiarity, much like meeting up with an old friend.

A float completes the scene in a way that other methods simply cannot, a fact described so perfectly by Ted Hughes in *Poetry in the Making.*

> *Your whole being rests lightly on your float, but not drowsily: very alert, so that the least twitch of the float arrives like an electric shock. And you are not only watching the float. You are aware, in a horizonless and slightly mesmerized way, like listening to the double bass in orchestral music, of fish below there in the dark.*

Of course, having opted to use a float, the next issue is which float to use and the key is to find one that is not just functional and suited to the job in hand, but also pleasing on the eye.

There is no shame in becoming attached to a float - particularly a hand-made quill - and such an attachment can also make life easier on the bank. Not only will the shotting pattern be etched in the mind but familiarity also helps when spotting the shyest of bites - or determining the nibble of a fish from a weed frond brushing the line or a water vole flicking the float rubber.

Last winter, the one surviving fledgling from our local pair of buzzards succumbed to starvation in the cold but I opted against burying him (at least other beasts would make use of his demise) and instead pinched a few primaries from which I made some floats. Nothing too special, but perfect tools for this summer's crucian fishing, being slender and sensitive - perfect for those shyest biting of fishes.

I first used one on Opening Day, and knowing the float's origins meant that even when it wasn't disappearing I still felt compelled to smile.

Chapter Four

First Cast

Life can only be understood backwards; but it must be lived forwards.
SØREN KIERKEGAARD

With everything readied, it is time for the angler to pause and breathe in the moment.

Observe the scene; tune into the birdsong; feel the air against your skin.

Here is a spell that you are not about to break, but hopefully meld into.

Too often the eagerness to wet a line forces a clumsy cast or heavy footfall, and not only might the fish have fled, but the whole day becomes disjointed and slightly alien.

The sense of being may be the angler's greatest weapon, but it is also the toughest to harness and most easy to lose. Like a first kiss, the first cast can lead you happily along a path of adventure, or leave you dry-mouthed and disillusioned.

Arthur Ransome wrote of the fear and excitement of the first cast of the season in *Rod and Line*. He describes how, when taking out his fly-rod at the start of a new season, he fears he has forgotten everything previously learned; so much so that he would always prefer to make his first cast of a new season in private.

Ransome feels that a first cast should never bring too much success, and that an angler should enjoy three separate miracles when making his first cast of the day. First, his line should land soft and straight. Then, secondly, his fly will rise a fish, though it is important that he misses the strike for the hooking of a trout should occur as the third miracle.

Ransome emphasises the importance of his second and third miracles occurring separately, which is an interesting philosophy. Missing a bite, or rise, can be a more valuable result of a first cast than actually catching a fish. It proves that the bait is attractive and that there are fish willing to feed, but it also reminds you of the appreciation for what you are doing. If the first cast resulted each time with your target prize then any sense of achievement would vanish, even on the occasion when the first cast might be your only cast.

There are situations while chasing wary fish when time on the bank is better spent building the quarry's confidence and not actually fishing. Steady baiting can convince a fish that all is safe and well and once fear is lost to a need to eat then a cast can be made. Even now though, and despite the hard work already put in, if the trick were to work every time then one's interest would soon be lost.

What the first cast does do is connect or reconnect you with that other world. Water is simply water until a fishing line links your conscious mind with the life within it. And though much is learned through time and observation, until you actually wet a line the final few pieces of the jigsaw simply do not fit.

With the first cast comes a dramatic shift of intensity. The world that moments earlier stretched to the far bank or down to that distant run of willows is now wholly peripheral. Instead, your vision and thoughts are tunnelled into that tight little area where your bait now lies.

As time passes without a bite so your focus will broaden slightly, involving your senses in the immediate area once more. Did that lily pad just move? Was that a swirl beside the reed-bed?

Some anglers, particularly those targeting carp, will spend time building a mental picture of every feature or undulation of the lake-bed that lies before them. They will cast around with leads in order to 'feel' what the bottom is made up of, and will use plummets or indicator floats to measure the depths of all the water within casting distance.

Ultimately, these anglers begin to see the lake or river as though there is no actual water there. The images they have in mind (and often put on to paper) are of the complete topography of the world into which they cast.

This practice is hugely beneficial if you are fishing for a small head of fish over a period of time. Knowing exactly what lies beneath the surface can give a vital edge as to plotting exactly where to place a bait.

Alternatively, you can rely a little more on good fortune and the skills learned in reading the water. The world around your float will be sending a steady stream of messages for you to decipher. Many of these messages will be either too subtle to read or blatant red herrings, but the intensity of awareness that is experienced with the first cast of the day often dictates the course of the day itself.

What is reassuring is how often the very spot that you chose to place your first cast is the very spot where you will want to cast subsequently.

Despite Arthur Ransome's suggestion of the need for separate miracles, there are occasions when the first cast brings a bite from the biggest fish of the day - particularly when targeting predatory species such as pike, perch or chub. These fish are more prone to a reaction of basic instinct than those species that spend their lives looking over their shoulder. Contrary to the oft quoted and entirely false 'goldfish with a seven second memory' mantra, fish do learn and have sufficient intelligence with which to develop their behaviour in accordance to specific events. Of course in centuries past, such as Ransome's day, a fish would only get to make one mistake. Until relatively recently the notion of returning a fish to the water was unheard of unless it was either undersize or inedible. As a result fish were far less tackle shy, but the instinctual behaviour of certain fish will not have changed at all in the years since.

The chub, for instance, is a lover of snags and undercuts, anywhere that he has cover above his head. As with the trout that my childhood self had watched in the Candover Stream, the biggest chub in the shoal will take up the prime positions within the stream. Not necessarily obvious to the angler, but a lie that is both safe, energetically economic and with optimum sight and reach of passing food. In such a situation, the biggest fish is often the first to move for a bait.

Izaak Walton demonstrated his awareness of this behaviour in *The Compleat Angler*.

> *Go to the same hole, where in most hot days you will finde floting neer the top of the water, at least a dozen or twenty Chubs; get a Grashopper or two as you goe, and get secretly behinde the tree, put it then upon your hook, and let your*

hook hang a quarter of a yard short of the top of the water,
and 'tis very likely that the shadow of your rod, which you
must rest on the tree, will cause the Chubs to sink down to
the bottom with fear; for they be a very fearful fish, and the
shadow of a bird flying over them will make them do so; but
they will presently rise up to the top again, and there lie
soaring till some shadow affrights them again: when they lie
upon the top of the water, look out the best Chub, which
you setting your self in a fit place, may very easily do, and
move your Rod as softly as a Snail moves, to that Chub you
intend to catch; let your bait fall gently upon the water three
or four inches before him, and he will infallibly take the
bait, and you will be as sure to catch him;

Though Walton describes how he would identify and single out
the biggest chub in the shoal, it is often the case that even when
you cannot see the fish the first chub will still be the best of
the day.

The same rule can be applied to perch which, like the chub,
will shoal in similar year groups. Obviously these shoals are
thinned by predation, disease and old age until fewer and fewer
fish remain. Without the intense competition of life within a
large shoal, the older fish benefit from an increase in availabil-
ity of food, and will in turn grow larger still. Allied to the fact
that the older fish are also those with the most intelligence and
certainly the strongest instincts of stealth and fear, the resulting
shoal members will be wily and suspicious. Still, however, the
perch is a creature of reaction, liable to respond to a baited hook
with an instinctive grab before he has considered whether or not
he has been deceived. With this in mind, if fishing for perch,

particularly big perch, then Ransome's premise should be totally disregarded. Focus wholly on hitting a bite on your first cast because it may well result in the biggest fish in the swim.

This point was proved to me last winter on a trip to the Dorset Stour.

I had arranged to meet Chris for a few casts on the second Wednesday of the New Year, but he telephoned on the prior Sunday with a change of plan.

"I'm going to have to fish tomorrow," he almost whispered, "I have a feeling . . ."

Tomorrow was Monday and I had loose plans, but Chris' feelings should never be dismissed. In 1980 he had a feeling on the eve of Opening Day and posted a couple of cards to his brother Nick and friend Rick telling them that he was going to catch a record carp at Redmire Pool the following day. The record had stood for twenty-eight years so such a feeling would be easily dismissed but it came true with a fish of 51½lb.

I juggled my Monday plans and arranged to meet Chris on the bank at mid-morning. Conditions could not have been much better.

The night-time temperature had barely dipped into single figures, and the low cloud cover that had given the mild air was set to remain all day. Low light levels are loved by all fish, but predators, such as the perch we would be chasing, are particularly stimulated. It is not unusual for perch to sit unmoved for hours on end until the sun dips and the fading light stirs their hunting instinct.

On one trip to the upper Kennet, my friend Martin found a lumpy perch laid up in a small weed-bed in around two feet of water. The fish seemed almost comatose and oblivious to our presence, so Martin proceeded to try and catch it. A worm, even when placed on the perch's nose, failed to stir any response, and instead Martin lowered in a small plastic lure on his jig rod. After some minutes of light jigging, the perch lazily took the bait. On lifting the rod tip, however, Martin found that the perch was merely gripping the tail of the lure and it promptly let go as soon as it neared the surface and returned to its original lie.

Over the course of two further hours, Martin had two further reactions from the fish, the second of which saw him finally hook it on a piece of worm. Such persistence deserved greater fortune than for the hook to ping out as the perch (which would have been his best ever) neared the landing-net.

It was a fascinating passage of events that demonstrated just how affected perch are by light conditions. With the sun overhead, the fish was utterly disinterested and it was not until shadow fell across its eyes that it showed any real willingness to feed.

On the upper Stour, the heavy sky was perfect for our wishes, and with only four feet or so of water this was of particular importance. Cormorants and otters are active hunters on this stretch of river, and the perch tend to hug the deeper central channel of the river in bright or clear water conditions.

On the bank where we stood ran a line of alders, overhanging the water and offering an element of shelter as well as plenty of shadow. My swim, the 'Standard swim' as Chris has christened it, offered a crease around a rod-length and a half out, which ran for around ten yards before nudging into a tangle of roots of the downstream tree. Those roots were an obvious holding spot, yet I had fished the swim before and found that the perch would patrol up and down the entire swim with no obvious pattern.

Chris himself was fishing 'Sub-standard' - a tight, intimate swim downstream from me. It was a spot easily overlooked, and certainly rarely fished, and the crowd of branches that surrounded him on three sides meant any fish would have to be played with care and control.

A few weeks earlier Sub-standard had given Chris a catch of four 2lb perch in less than an hour topped off by a fish which was a couple of drams under three pounds, so he was more than happy to let me fish the more consistent upstream spot.

In my previous trip a fortnight prior, I had also caught well, with a brace and a half of 2-pounders, the first of which came on just my second cast.

With that in mind, I was well aware that my first cast might just produce a fish.

I trickled a light stream of maggots into the head of the swim for about twenty minutes before casting, hoping to stir up the minnows and roach and maybe get any resident perch bristling. I knew the depth from my previous visit, and in fact had the shotted float and line still intact in my coat* pocket.

I broke a couple of worms into pieces and let them sink along the crease before baiting the hook (half a worm and two maggots) and swinging the float out into the flow.

It travelled no more than three feet before bobbing sharply. I thought, briefly, that it may have been an over-exuberant minnow, but it dragged slowly away to the right in classic perch fashion.

I lifted the rod and bent into solid resistance, immediately regretting my choice of hook size.

I had opted for a size 12 tied to 3lb 6oz breaking strain line, a decision based on the low, clear water and a sense that the fish might respond best to a relatively small bait. Perch have large mouths, and a bunch of lobworms on a size 2 can be engulfed by a pounder, but sometimes they will shy away from big mouthfuls and instead are tempted by small baits.

Now though, with a large, angry fish shaking its head beneath my rod tip, I was painfully aware of how light a hook hold a size 12 might give.

I let the fish work out into the main current, allowing the rod (the split-cane Avocet) to absorb as much of the power as I felt it could without pinging the hook free.

It was a nervy few moments, not helped by my first glimpse of the fish. It was a big perch - possibly a 3-pounder.

It dived again but without the power this time - steady Kev, steady.

I went with the net a little too keenly and nearly made a bodge of it, the fish making a surge for the roots beneath my feet and underneath the net. Too often I have lost fish at this

---

*A coat dedicated solely for fishing purposes is a vital part of the Idle Angler's armoury. It will inevitably become dirty and smelly, factors which while rendering the wearer a social pariah, do allow him/her to operate within their chosen pastime with greater, more natural harmony.

While warmth and weatherproofing are desirable properties, of equal importance is the presence of cavernous, well secured pockets. These should be deep enough to store terminal tackle, a water bottle, some sandwiches, scales, forceps, floats, and a centre-pin reel - giving easy access during the course of a day.

Vitally though, at the end of the day when it is too dark to see the float and your journey home does not need to be overly hindered by the painful practice of packing up, the end tackle can simply be bitten off and buried in a coat pocket - ready to use next time.

moment but not this time, and after one more sub-surface circle he was in the net and mine.

"That's a three . . ." Chris murmured from behind my shoulder.

The hook, a barbless, came out in the net and Chris did the honours with the scales, taunting me at first with a groan of disappointment before turning the dial to show a weight of 3lb 8oz. A new personal best - by just a single ounce. I did not cast again for an hour and truthfully would not have been upset to have headed home without re-wetting the line.

I did of course, and went on to catch another three perch, though none as big as the first.

As much as that first cast resulted in utter success, I have made countless more that have ended in minor disaster, normally due to over-exuberance. As a child, all that mattered was getting a bait into the water, and every second used testing knots or plumbing the depth was time wasted. I wouldn't consider any of the pitfalls of rushing to cast, and would regularly tangle in branches behind me or overhead before even wetting a line. At such moments my impetuousness would replace straight-forward impatience and rather than making sensible effort to free the line, I would either worsen the tangle or snap the line with an angry flick of the rod tip.

Such moments are to be learned from while growing up, but such would be my excitement to cast that I would make the same mistake again and again. If I actually managed to make a cast, then it would be adrenaline fuelled and would sail into a lily bed or duck house.

I didn't help myself by existing in that naïve world (in which I snapped my first ever rod) where the further one casts the more fish he will catch, but such follies are not to be rued. It is those elementary mistakes which lead you toward a more ful-filling understanding of fish and fishing, and without them nothing can ever be learned.

Far too many anglers today inhibit their own development by succumbing to the temptation of instant angling.

Baits which can stay solid and active for days are attached to ready made rigs that are cast into overstocked lakes. At some point, almost regardless of where a cast is made, a fish will pick up the bait and hook itself. By playing the law of averages these anglers will at some point hook a large fish and consider them-selves to be successful anglers. While they may well find all of the satisfaction they need from such a routine, it seems sad that 'success' can be so easily achieved.

We often consider what makes a 'good' angler and against what such merit should be measured. There are fishermen who are phenomenally good at catching big fish, others at catching lots of fish, but none could be so content on the riverbank as my late grandfather, who was happy enough to puff on his pipe and watch his float drift around a slow eddy without ever going under. He would go home fishless but totally happy, and in such a state of mind how could he not be considered a success-ful angler?

I spent an afternoon last winter fishing for perch on the estate lake near the cottage, knowing that there might only be two perch in an acre of water. The fact that they might have been there provided enough excuse to put up a rod with a favourite quill on a beautiful late season day. I loved every second, and as I made my first cast I was incredibly aware of possibility. With this being a water where I had only ever surface-fished for carp, it was as though I were fishing it for the first time.

Some first casts, even on virgin water, can deliver gut-churning disappointment.

A family holiday aboard a boat on the Shannon offered one of the more painful. Fishing opportunities were limited to dawn and dusk and stops for lunch, and though I caught plenty of fish I hadn't had the opportunity to fill a net with the big bream that made the Shannon system famous. The final day was to give me that chance though, as we arrived back in Athlone early and I had the whole afternoon to fish the Meadows stretch below the town.

It was a renowned stretch of water, and in the 1980s offered some of the best bream fishing in Ireland with matches turning up enormous catches of fish.

This was the Ireland that I really fancied a taste of and as I made my way downstream from the town bridge I could see two anglers fishing and both were into fish.

They had recast by the time I reached them but in no time the tip on the downstream angler's rod tweaked round and he was into another bream. It was a good fish, over five pounds, and I learned that they had been fishing here all week, albeit in a different peg each day, and the fishing had been extraordinary.

"It doesn't matter where you go," they explained, "just put a load of groundbait in a third of the way across and fish over the top - the bream will turn up sooner rather than later."

I took myself another hundred yards or so downstream and did as they suggested. I had a fair bit of bait left and threw in most of it, leaving sufficient for three or four hours feeder fishing.

As I lined up the first cast my confidence almost bubbled over. This was inevitable. It was just a matter of time. The swimfeeder hit the water directly over the groundbaited area and I feathered the line waiting for it to hit bottom. It didn't.

I had managed to find the only weed-bed along the stretch and throw all my bait straight into it. I lost my feeder on that first cast, and tied on a lead, hoping to find a clear spot but there were none. Then, to compound matters, I slipped on the bank and fell on to my reel, snapping off the handle. I didn't have a spare.

Fortunately, casting into virgin waters is normally less traumatic, though any moments that are memorable for whatever reason are worth experiencing, no matter how frustrating at the time.

What is essential with a first cast is to appreciate the anticipation of it and then absorb yourself within it. It is a short burst of Christmas Eve and New Season Eve rolled into one and no matter what happens thereafter those emotions will remain.

It is interesting that my most memorable first cast came not as a child, nor when fishing new hallowed water, but was instead on a water I fished regularly and in a swim I had cast many times before.

The previous week, a dozen of us met on the banks of the river Kennet for what was to be a social gathering as much as a feast of angling.

I had got there early with Martin and found the main river up, cold and coloured - far from ideal. I winkled out a chub before exploring some of the feeder streams which were carrying less water than the main channels and one of which I knew would be holding some fish. For most of the year this piece of water would appear no more than a ditch, but it would swell in winter and an array of small fish would find refuge here away from the main flow. It was easily overlooked and very lightly

71

fished, but I had seen roach over two pounds tucked up in the past and in one particular spot had lost the biggest perch that I had ever seen.

It was there I headed, and the undisturbed banks suggested no one had wet a line there all season. A trickle of maggots got a few fish moving, and I hooked a dace and two small roach before bending into a perch well over a pound. Another perch followed before I headed back to the fishing hut for lunch.

With all expected parties now arrived, lunch became a pro-longed affair as people acquainted and reacquainted themselves. Ben had brought a crate of ale and the conversations flowed.

Nobody had caught much, except Peter who knows the Kennet as well as any man, so news of my fairly modest success was greeted with great interest and by mid-afternoon half a dozen rods were poking through the tangle of the ditch.

Jon and Ben found some good perch further upstream, but the hotspot was definitely the snag swim where I had spent the morning and Chris was happily plundering the perch. His third fish was a 2-pounder, and he soon added three more above that weight, with the best just shy of three pounds.

As people began to gather for a cup of tea and football updates, Chris insisted that he vacate the swim but with so many present, and not one of them comfortable with fishing the pool at another's expense, it was eventually decided to take turns.

A couple of radios were tuned to Radio Solent (for the foot-ball commentary) and the kettles were stoked up again, while one by one we took our chance to hook a perch.

As the fish kept coming, so did the goals, with Southampton rattling in five against Tranmere Rovers. With each event came a louder cheer and by the time the float melted into the darkness of night, we all wore smiles as wide as a goalmouth.

Inside, I was smiling even more broadly though, for I had been invited back to fish the same stretch the following week and I would have the pool to myself.

I went to sleep that evening to a blur of stripes and possibility. If I could have returned the next day I would have, but knew that a week's rest would give the perch time to settle and in the meantime I would satisfy myself with the visualisation of a bobbing float.

The swim itself had responded best to float fished worm, inched down to the snag where it could be gently held back, the bait fluttering up into the perch lair. As each workday passed, the thought of my first cast the following weekend became ever more etched into my thoughts.

I knew the swim would not be fished in the meantime, one of the joys of fishing private water, but the conditions could be all important. If the river level dropped then the fish might move back out into the main stream, whereas bright sunshine could cause major problems in such a shallow, narrow piece of water.

Each lunchtime was spent gathering worms, until I had sufficient to feed the whole river, and each night I was finding it tougher and tougher to sleep.

By the time Saturday night arrived, I was so charged with anticipation that I could only manage a few fitful hours in bed and ended up getting up and heading for the river well before dawn.

I couldn't fish until my host arrived at about nine o'clock, but struck up the kettle and readied the rod so that when he arrived, I could simply shake his hand and make for the side-stream.

The weather was cooler but the breeze was a westerly and would be peppering my back should it rain, so I should be comfortable enough.

In order not to spook any resident fish, I climbed a couple of fences in order to approach the swim from above. A couple of snipe zig-zagged away from beneath my feet and when I was about ten yards from the water I laid down the bulk of my tackle, taking just my rod, net and tub of worms into position. A couple of broken worms were allowed to drift down on the current before the moment of truth arrived. It was a peculiar sensation, being right there in a moment I had rehearsed so many times over the past seven days and for a couple of moments I paused. Did I really want to make this real? Could I cope if, after so much anticipation, nothing happened?

Deep breath, swing the bait into the flow and hold the float back to let it swing into line.

All good, now I just had to let the float inch down to the raft above the lair. It took ten seconds or so to ride the current but it seemed to take an age, and yet the float looked as though it belonged. The way it sat in the water, pulled steadily along by bait and shot below. As it reached the snag I gently tightened up and held the float in perfect position.

For a moment I thought I had imagined the bob, but there was no mistaking the dragging bite that followed. They were still there - it was going to be a good day.

Chapter Five

Lunchtime

Time is an illusion. Lunchtime doubly so.
DOUGLAS ADAMS, THE HITCHHIKER'S GUIDE TO THE GALAXY

I cannot recall his name, but do remember that he had moved to England from Bosnia and that he was held in high esteem in his homeland for his writing ability. So much so that he still wrote for angling publications in his homeland even though the nature of his articles might seem rather incongruous with a western bent.

Once he and I had discovered our shared passion, we would talk fishing whenever our paths crossed and almost inevitably the main topic of conversation would come back to the British habit that puzzled him the most. We put the fish back.

Not all captures get to swim again, of course. Game and sea fish are regularly taken for the pot, though in both branches conservation is given far more emphasis than in the past.

The demise of the Atlantic salmon is well documented and as a result restrictions are placed upon the amount of fish that can be taken. Moreover, the fishermen themselves are aware of the salmon's plight and will discern to return a vast majority of the fish that they would be entitled to take.

Similarly, sea anglers are keen to promote the preservation of marine stocks. It seems so unlikely that man could have fished the seas so dry, but such is the efficiency of commercial nets that many species are simply not sustainable.

The modern sea angler is far more concerned with conservation than personal triumph, and fish that were once routinely kept are now returned. Even record sized fish are put back, despite the fact that the weighing of a fish must take place on dry, stable land in order for it to be ratified. Such is the awareness among anglers, though, that the angler returning such a catch earns as much respect and kudos from his peers than any person whose name is etched in the official record books. Further more, some fish, particularly sharks and skate, are often tagged and records made in order to aid species conservation.

We have become a nation aware of nature's fragility and of how great our impact can be upon it, but perhaps we are treating the symptoms instead of finding a cure. Any river in full health should be able to support sufficient stocks for the otters, herons, kingfishers and people to take their share. A balanced habitat will always function best with predators and prey, and though it is for good reason that we have adapted our habits as anglers, perhaps as a nation we should be looking deeper.

All this conjecture is of little consequence to my Bosnian friend, however. Back home, he was taught to fish in order to provide food for the table and the species most familiar to him were in Britain described as 'coarse'.

"They are not coarse," he would always argue, "they are delicious!"

He would describe the methods of cooking all sorts of species and nothing would go to waste - not even the tiddlers. These fish, primarily small roach and rudd, would be gutted and but-terflied before being coated in seasoned flour and flash fried. Delicious apparently, though I struggled to consider such fish for their culinary virtues. Deep-fried battered anything can taste all right but that is due to the cooking process and I couldn't help but feel that a dainty little roach would get lost among the salt, pepper and fat.

Obviously my mind has been conditioned to see certain fish as unpalatable, though this discretion is accentuated by the abuse that my senses have received when catching them. The smell of a tench from a deep, silty pond is evocative but in no way pleasant. Here is a fish that filters years of rank detritus and whose flesh is surely methanol stained. Add to that the slime and I fail to believe Izaak Walton's assertion 'that he eats pleas-antly'.

For Walton though, his angle came very much from the direction of my Bosnian friend. He would go a' angling very much with food in mind, and *The Compleat Angler* was written accordingly, with emphasis placed upon a fish's edibility as much as its sporting quality.

Even the humble bleak gets a mention in culinary terms, though one wonders if it is with a strong helping of seasoning.

There is no better sport then whipping for Bleaks in a boat in a Summers evening, with a hazle top about five or six foot long, and a line twice the length of the Rod. I have heard Sir Henry Wotton say, that there be many that in Italy will catch Swallows so, or especially Martins (the Bird-Angler standing on the top of a Steeple to do it, and with a line twice so long, as I have spoke of) and let me tell you,

*Scholer, that both Martins and Blekes be most excellent
meat.*

Nevertheless, I have it on sound authority that Walton's opinion of the bream - that it is taken to be more pleasant or
sweet than wholesome - is spot on.

Many years ago, an acquaintance caught a four pound bream
from the Royalty stretch of the Hampshire Avon, and found it
to be deeply hooked. The hook in question was large, having
carried a massive lump of luncheon-meat intended for a barbel,
and sadly was beyond the reach of a disgorger. The fish was also
bleeding from the gills and the most humane action was to
euthanise it.

Not wanting the fish to have died for nothing, he took the
bream home and baked it - and he was astonished by the
results.

'Better than sea bream', is how the taste was described to me,
which is high praise indeed. Admittedly this fish did come from
the clean, sparkling waters of the Avon and a similar fish
from a mere or estate lake would surely be muddy in compari-
son - and I doubt it tasted quite as good as he claimed, for he
has not 'deep-hooked' one since.

But why all this talk of fish as food? It must be lunchtime . . .

As a child I never worried about lunch when I went fishing.
Until lunchtime.

There were always other things to concern myself with on a
fishing day, principally getting to the water as soon as possible
so I could send my first cast into a tree.

Short-termism is a trait shared among all children, and one
that isn't all bad. The ability to care for nothing more than the

moment you are in is a quality lost too easily in adulthood.

But while living in the moment might benefit the soul, your stomach does not always appreciate it, and mine used to grumble noisily on the riverbank. Normally, the only way to ease the growls was to delve into my bait bag and that was far from satisfactory. My mother used to buy the driest brown bread in existence on the pretence that it was 'healthy', and of the few slices in my bag I could only ever eat the crusts because I might need the soft bit for bait. A swig of water might have aided my mastication, but there had been no time to think about food that morning, let alone a drink.

Instead I would either gack my mouth together or dunk the crusts into sweetcorn juice - if I had a tin of the golden grains. Alternatively luncheon-meat might be on the menu; the greasiness would make the bread more digestible but the saltiness really didn't help my thirst.

Worse still came as the result of delving in my brother's bait bag. He had always fancied carp fishing and despite the fact that they were uncatchable in Alresford Pond (a legend he one day disproved) he bought himself a suitable rod and a bag of the new 'wonder' bait - boilies.

They smelt amazing - a lovely sweet vanilla - and it seemed inconceivable that they would taste anything other than yellow bonbons without the dusting of icing sugar. As it transpired they were all but inedible. The taste was so intense that my mouth frothed and foamed - those things were drier than Oscar Wilde.

At least in late summer and autumn there is some food to be found in the hedgerows. Blackberries are the obvious favourite and they were unmistakably safe in my eyes, saving a young angler from starvation on more than one occasion.

Ultimately, though, I just had to learn the importance of taking food with me - especially in winter. The cold draws your energy as a leach draws blood, and food is ever more important. A packed lunch did eventually become a fixture of my (mental) pre-trip checklist, though for many years the actual process of eating remained a hindrance.

It is a well noted phenomenon that the float will go under the moment an angler reaches for a lunchbag or takes a sip of tea. The debate as to whether it is an awareness on the fish's part or straightforward coincidence has been discussed enough else-where, but for myself it simply proved that giving the art anything other than a hundred per cent of my attention would lead to a missed opportunity.

Perhaps if my first outings beside a river were with a fly-rod then I might have learned sooner the advantage of treating lunchtime as a rather pleasant diversion within the whole day. It is very nearly impossible to cast a fly and eat simultaneously, so a fly angler will reel in his line, lay down his rod and actually enjoy his lunch.

Having said that, the point should also be made that the fly-angler can be as loathe to lose precious angling time as his coarse contemporary.

Arthur Ransome wrote fondly of Fishing Inns, but decreed that the fishing available at such a hostelry could be determined by what they served for lunch.

A fishing inn would often control the rights of a nearby river, though Ransome felt that if they offered luncheon then it was surely a sign that the fishing was poor. After all, the guests would surely want to dash out of the door after breakfast with a packet of sandwiches in their pocket and the hope that sport would be so good that they would not think of food until the sun was setting.

Sadly, though a few still remain, the role of the fishing inn is no longer part of our angling convention. I have always loved the idea of spending a few days at a riverside pub - fishing by day and enjoying ales beside the fire of an evening. Arthur Applin stoked this fantasy in his book *Philandering Angler*, in which he described fondly his stays at The Carnarvon Arms on the edge of Exmoor.

He would rise brown trout on the Exe, before returning to the pub where, if his day was successful, his catch would be cooked for his supper. The pub itself is no more, surviving at least for a few decades more than the railway beside which it was originally built to serve. The demise of the railways in the 1960s coincided with the construction of motorways and the accessibility of the motor car, and the role of riverside inns altered accordingly. No longer were they destinations to be reached by rail, the journey itself necessitating the need for full or half board. Modern day anglers could eat up the miles by road and take themselves to ever more remote pools. The inn of Ransome and Applin's day would now only ever receive anglers looking for a light lunch - the very thing that Ransome felt such places should not offer and a provision for which the inn itself could not profit from for long.

In this age of convenience anglers are even less likely to make use of local facilities, unless these facilities come to them. Some commercial fisheries offer more than just guaranteed sport from tidy platforms and well kept banks. On-site cafés will offer all-day breakfasts or bacon rolls delivered to your swim. Mobile telephones give long-stay anglers the chance to order pizza, curry or whatever might take their fancy without reeling in. And they can enjoy whatever is delivered safe in the knowledge that a bite alarm will sing should a fish take their bait.

Such instant, canned succour divides as much opinion as the style of fishing to which it best serves, but if someone takes enjoyment from their own angle then there can be no wrong within it. Moreover the chance to drive a car to one's swim and have a safe, secure platform on which to fish allows many of those people less able to still enjoy their sport.

For those anglers seeking out the challenge and solitude from the wilder reaches of our rivers, sustenance is not only useful as a fuel for the body, it can also provide a break for the mind.

As your first cast drew your attention tight into a single area of consequence, so your awareness of the overall picture became veiled. To actually stop and withdraw can open up your eyes again and enable you to see things slightly differently.

I like to feed a little more loose feed than I have been and then remove myself from the swim I have been fishing in order to take lunch. I might strike up the kettle - though tea-time will warrant a chapter later of its own - but most vitally, I will let my senses relax from the intensity of my angling and re-tune to hear what songs are played elsewhere.

If the fish have been feeding, then I may have little more need than to eat my food, flex my fingers and carry on catching. Such times are rare though and it is unusual for there to be nothing to do that might improve the day.

Conditions will have changed. The sun may be warmer, the wind direction different. If bites have tailed off then perhaps it is because the light levels have increased - pushing the fish towards cover. If the air temperature has risen then the fish may have moved accordingly, seeking out the shallower water which is the quickest to warm.

It is feasible that you may have exhausted your swim, caught all the fish that it may offer, and but for the break now to consider that fact, you might have found yourself scratching for bites all afternoon.

Are there any subtle alterations you could make to your tackle? A smaller hook perhaps - lighter line - or a change of bait?

Such thoughts seem obvious and will be turning around in your mind all the while you are fishing, but time passes in a peculiar fashion while staring at a float and the anxiety created by so many anomalies can create an unpleasant focus.

Far better to clear your head of all the puzzlements and fish on, be it where you are or in a new location, with a mind more receptive to the water.

Ultimately, an angler's aim is to unshackle from constraints of time and simply be. There is music playing wherever you turn an ear, and the more you involve and immerse, the clearer the tune will become.

If your tackle is safe then lunchtime is also a great time to leave it where it lays and have a stroll. You will have most likely explored when first arriving, but much could have changed in the few hours since, and a fresh view might reveal secrets that were previously hidden.

It is good to get the joints moving too, loosen up and stretch your legs. I know of no anglers that have fallen victim to deep vein thrombosis but have no intention of being the first. My posture is never the best, but I will happily distort my body for hours on end when fishing. Pins and needles can drift dangerously close to paralysis before I move myself and shake life back into my limbs.

When I smoked I would enjoy a cigarette now, safe in the knowledge that the glowing end would not end up somewhere it shouldn't. Smoking while fishing can be risky, as my friend Hugh once discovered.

After some years of perseverance, I felt I had pretty much cracked the roach in Alresford Pond. If conditions were right, then I could take half a dozen before the shoal would spook - and these were big fish, all around 1½ to 1¾ lb with the odd 2lb warrior.

Hugh had cycled down to see me on the Pond one evening just as I got them feeding and stood wide-eyed as I caught a string of lumpy roach. I soon had just one pinch of bread left, and offered Hugh the rod - he would surely obliterate his personal best.

The float soon bobbed and slid away, but Hugh struck into thin air. For a moment, I stood perplexed - I could still see the float sinking deeper and deeper but Hugh was striking repeatedly and nothing was happening. Then the pieces fell into place. Hugh was holding the rod in his right hand with a cigarette between his fingers. The embers had melted the line just above the reel and to make matters worse, the severed twist of monofilament was just coiling through the tip ring. I made a dive but was too late, though fortunately for the fish, it didn't hook itself as the float resurfaced and I was able to retrieve the whole lot on my next visit.

Though it is many years since I smoked I do have a fondness

for a drink, though alcohol is something I very rarely enjoy on the riverbank.

There are odd occasions when a bottle of real ale might fall out of someone's bag and I will enjoy every sip, but as a rule they are pleasures that I prefer not to mix.

I like the clarity of thought that is gained while fishing and the buzz of booze can numb the senses and leave you with something missing.

On the flipside, there are occasions when the fishing itself is secondary to the social aspect of the day. Old friends may meet for a day by the water and carrying a rod merely gives a purpose for being there.

One of my favourite fishing lunches came some years ago on the banks of the river Test - and I enjoyed more than one drink that day.

Sir John Whitaker Fairclough was a man I never met but whose fly-fishing tackle is now in my possession.

Fairclough was a key developer of IBM's System 360 computers in the 1960s, machines that set industry standards in the era of mainframe computing.

His reputation grew and in 1986 he was appointed Chief Scientific advisor to Margaret Thatcher's Tory government. Fairclough's business-like approach and attitude to British scientific research may have divided opinion amongst his peers but certainly suited Conservative attitudes.

During his tenure he was called on to address issues away from his own field of expertise, such as the fall-out from the Chernobyl disaster and the future of Britain's own nuclear power industry.

When he died in 2003, his memorial service at St Martin in

the Fields was attended by Royalty and Heads of State, but it was for other reasons that I learned of him.

I worked in a garage at the time, and regular customers Dr and Mrs Baits were friends with the recently late Fairclough and his widow. Among other duties (such as organising the memorial service) they were charged with finding a home for Sir John's fishing jacket. They knew I was a fisherman and asked if I would like it. I gratefully accepted and was amazed to receive not just a jacket, but also a fly rod, reels and two boxes of flies.

Despite living in chalkstream-rich Hampshire, my experiences of fly casting were, up to then, pretty much zero, and I became a little anxious as to where I could test out my newly acquired gear. I have never been a particularly good pupil - preferring instead to teach myself and give-up fairly quickly if I am clearly no good at it but was also aware of how embarrassed I might feel making virgin attempts in front of seasoned fluff-chuckers.

Then came an email that solved my dilemma. Nell's god-father owned a stretch of the Test near Chilbolton and had offered it to her and husband Jules for a day of their choosing. Did I, and fellow friend Ron, care to join them?

This was perfect, not only for the pleasure of seeing old friends, but also because all four of us were fly-fishing tyros. Ron had some experience having caught plenty of trout in the past and is also the last person in the world who would mock anyone else's inabilities.

Ron picked me up on a lovely late July morning and we made the short journey to the river where we met our hosts.

From the cars we headed south, through a couple of meadows

and some thick undergrowth, before the roof of a salmon hut appeared above the reeds with the Test sparkling just behind.

Half a mile of river was ours, though in truth we had walked far enough from any roads or buildings to feel that we owned the whole of the stream. It is always a wonder in such isolation as to how a building such as the salmon hut here was constructed. This was not just any old hut either, it had two rooms, comfy sofas and enough space for a party should we have wanted one.

There seemed no great rush to fish, for a while we were all content to poke around and breathe in the scene. It may have been mid-summer but there was still plenty of birdsong - dominated by the sedge warblers dotted among the reed-beds on either bank.

The breeze was a little stiffer than would have been ideal, novice casting is tough enough without the wind tangling your line. Fortunately though, in the hut were a couple of pairs of chest waders which meant we could get into the river itself and take the overhanging trees out of the casting equation. I booted up and worked my way slowly upstream, scattering a few trout and making a couple of half hearted casts before I saw Ron wading below me and hooking a fish on his first cast. It was a grayling - not a big one - but a fish on a fly. I waded down to see what he had caught it on, and to see if I had anything similar.

"Nothing special . . ." Ron suggested, offering his fly for inspection. He was right, I doubt this pattern had a name, it was just a wad of green on a big hook. Ron pulled a small bag from his pocket and passed it to me.

"Help yourself, Kev."

There were a dozen or so of the same pattern but in a variety of colours, all squeezed into a small plastic sleeve with a 99p price tag on the side.

My flies, all careful imitations, would have cost more than that each but Ron's presentation was clearly better than my own, as he proved by hooking a second grayling.

I snuck one of his glitzy specials into my fly box and worked further upstream to where the river swallowed slightly and a thin slip of island jutted up from the central channel.

There was a nice brownie lying immediately above the upstream point of the island, and though the overhanging undergrowth looked a likely place for my line to tangle, it also offered a bit of cover. I had a few practice casts below the fish, and got a feel of the distance I would need to find, and then fired my line right to the tip of its nose.

In a flash it rose and the line briefly tightened, but before I could react it had dropped limp and the fish had zig-zagged away upstream. Wow! I didn't care that I hadn't hooked it, the fact that I had risen it was prize enough, and though he spooked, he hadn't gone far; he would surely be back.

After fifteen minutes or so he returned. I didn't notice him come but he simply materialised in the exact same spot.

I didn't practise this time, just freed some line and twirled the rod and my impatience showed as I splatted the line just a few yards in front of me.

The trout remained though, and the next dozen casts were so inaccurate that they didn't come close to spooking him. Finally, I got it right and he rose again and this time I was ready, lifting the rod as he thumped his tail and shot off downstream.

The reel buzzed, but only briefly, as the line again went limp and my hopes were again thwarted. The hook seemed okay, certainly sharp enough, but that trout wasn't going to come back this time.

As I pondered my next move, a shout went up downstream. It was lunchtime.

I hadn't given food much thought through the morning, and certainly hadn't brought enough with me to share, but that mattered not, as the spread in the hut was incredible.

Jules and Nell had folded out a table and covered it with food. There were pastas, rice dishes, cold meats and olives and then in the middle were cheeses and fresh bread. A bottle of wine was already open and a second was waiting and all thoughts of lost fish and crap casting dissolved into a Rioja haze.

For maybe two hours we sat and ate and drank and laughed. Such is the liberation gained from fresh air and good company that though the alcohol may have loosened us a little, it was the circumstances that gave us so much to smile about.

We finished the wine outside in the sunshine as the air began to cloud with a hatch that the swallows and martins dived among. Glorious - and the fishing was not lost to the afternoon either, even if the weather changed.

I must have cast for one fish forty times, and tried every fly in the box in vain. Eventually the only fly left was Ron's kitsch special and I tied it on as raindrops began to fall and the first roll of thunder echoed through the valley.

It worked first cast, and this time I managed to bundle my first ever fly-caught brownie into the net. Judging by the shape of him he looked as though he needed a meal, but I still had to show him off, and ran back to the hut where the others were sensibly sheltering in order to give them a glimpse before I slipped him back to the river.

It had been a fabulous day, crowned by the catering and I couldn't care that the walk back was so sodden.

We rounded off the evening with a pint in the village pub, though the adventure did not end there for Jules and Nell.

Jules' car did not have a roof (I cannot recall the model but it may have been built in part by Jules himself) and with the rain still falling they could not drive home. Instead, they secured the car with a tarpaulin to keep out the worst of the weather and made back for the salmon hut with a blanket, another bottle and a rather enviable night beside the river with the a summer storm rumbling around them.

I bet they slept like stones.

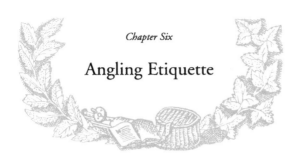

Chapter Six

Angling Etiquette

'If you're lonely when you're alone, you're in bad company.'
JEAN-PAUL SARTRE

Swelling Hill pond lies in central Hampshire between the villages of Ropley and Four Marks on the top of the hill from where it takes its name. Though it served as a water supply for Four Marks before the local homes became mains supplied, the small half-acre pool became neglected and by the early 1970s was silted and overgrown.

A local initiative to restore the pond was begun in 1975, and a damn fine job they did too, not least in providing local children with a venue on which to fish.

I first fished it in the mid Eighties, inspired by playground rumours that suggested it was possible to catch in excess of half a dozen fish in an afternoon.

After a gruelling first season on Alresford Pond, during which I managed to catch a grand total of nine fish (4 tench, 2 roach, 2 eels, and 1 perch) the prospect of a pond where I wouldn't have to wait ten hours for a bite seemed utopian, even if the prizes were mainly stunted little roach or rudd.

Moreover, I paid five pounds a season to struggle for bites on

Alresford when I could catch all day at Swelling Hill for free. The downside was that while Alresford was within cycling range, to venture further meant smiling sweetly at my parents for a lift.

This was an obstacle slightly eased as word got out at school that Swelling Hill was the centre of the fishing universe, and as more and more of us kids begged our parents for lifts, so more and more spare seats in cars became available.

There could be up to a dozen fisherboys casting into the pond on a Sunday afternoon, and inevitably among such number would come a bad egg or two.

Nothing too sinister went on, but it was the lack of etiquette that bothered me most. If I started to catch a few fish, then the swims around me would soon be filled. I could cope with this, but not the extreme actions of one particular kid I will call Charles.

Charles was crap at fishing and had no interest in learning, instead he would wait until someone else began getting bites and then sidle up next to them. He wouldn't just cast into the vicinity though and instead would aim his float directly at your own. Being a hopeless caster he would inevitably, at some point, tangle his line with your own.

He would then get in a mood, throw his rod to the ground and skulk off into the bushes for a sulk, leaving you to untangle the mess.

If it happened once or twice, then I could have coped with it, but Charles would always follow the same course of action. It wasn't long before I would up and move as soon as he arrived at my shoulder and lined up his cast, but he had no shame in following me wherever I went. Even the corner swim above the jetty, where it was impossible to fit two rods, was not safe. He would simply approach from the other side and cast back across at you.

Trips with Charles to Swelling Hill became ordeals, the only respite coming on those days when bites were so hard to come by that he would lose interest altogether and wander off to throw stones at cars. On other days when the fish were more obliging I would find myself stalling, casting without bait on, or not fishing altogether, all in the hope that he might take a wander and I could have an intensive twenty-minute angle.

Fortunately, as my patience was nearing its limit, Charles' parents decided to up sticks and move to a different county. I never heard from or saw him again, and I very much doubt he ever cast a line again. I have certainly encountered people like him through the years though, on the riverbank as well as in 'real' life.

I consider myself a sociable soul, and love nothing more than laughing hard in the company of friends, but I find it far too easy to get irked by the guy who parks his 4x4 across two spaces, or the woman who blocks the aisle with her shopping trolley.

These people are not deliberately targeting me - they are more likely thoughtless than downright rude, but it is that lack of consideration for others that is so hard to tolerate.

And when it comes to fishing, my private solitude, I have far less patience.

The vast majority of anglers are people worth knowing, and certainly offer value for conversation. After all, angling is as good an ice-breaker as the state of the weather, and a damn sight more interesting.

I met a chap out fishing with his young daughter last season on the Stour and we immediately struck up a conversation. His daughter who was only five or six years old, tugged at his sleeve a little nervously and asked, "Do you know this man, Daddy?"

He replied in the negative but explained that I was another fisherman and that all fishermen spoke to one another on the riverbank. She didn't buy it, and looked confused and suspicious. Not talking to strangers is not only an idiom aimed at children from the moment they emerge from the womb, it is also a habit that we maintain for our entire lives.

Holding a fishing rod, however, seems to offer licence for anyone within sight to enter into dialogue with you, and not just other anglers. If you cast near a bridge then it is inevitable that someone will walk across it and be immediately compelled to enquire as to your fortune. I don't mind this, and happen to think a more open attitude to my fellow man something of a liberation in a world that is often too precious, but there is often a difficulty with the wording of the reply. Do I reel off the diary of my morning's captures including every bleak and minnow when the questioner probably knows little of fish, or do I give an abrupt retort that might be considered surly. If I have to look away from my float in order to make this exchange (which is essential if I am to be heard above the sound of the stream and passing traffic) then I want to keep the words as brief as possible so as to not miss a bite. But should I talk without showing my face then my words will be lost on the wind and I will be forced to repeat myself.

It is a peculiar fact that some ninety-five per cent of people who ask questions from the top of bridges seem to be hard of hearing, and shouting while fishing is just wrong.

In time the angler learns to communicate with an undulatory pitch, raising his voice as he glances back at his float, but immediately lowering it as he turns back to face his fellow discourser offering a steady volume that is easy to discern. He also learns not to bamboozle a stranger with talk of stret-pegging and holding back hard, but also not to offer insult by only speaking in words of less than three syllables.

References to the weather or river level and the effect of them on you/your catch are easily recognised in lay terms and also offer the bridge walker an easy thread to pick up on. We all love to talk about the weather, but that person probably crosses the bridge often, if not daily, and will always look down upon the water.

Yes, they will agree, the river level has dropped considerably since the floods in October when the local gardens were underwater. That must have been awful you offer with sympathy - were they directly affected?

And suddenly you are the one asking the questions and in charge of the conversation. You can watch your float while nodding sagely as you hear all about Reg's champion pumpkins going rotten underwater just a week before the annual Gardening Awards and no bites will be missed and no offence will have been caused.

While human interaction on the riverbank will not necessarily improve your catches it may well benefit the soul. With so much of our lives filled with stresses and rigours that dominate our thoughts and conversations, the utter escapism that we feel while fishing can go unnoticed until we share it. We smile more when fishing, we relax and unwind and this is evident from our outward demeanour. Most people are routinely unaware of their actual selves, so hidden are they behind defensive walls placed to deflect self-criticism and potential failings. As a result we are guarded when we meet others, so conscious of causing offence or suffering ridicule that though the encounter may be perfectly amiable it is also strained.

While we perceive fishing as being a source of relief and release from our daily lives, particularly work or financial angst, it is actually a little deeper than that. We become truer to our selves when angling, more in tune with what truly shapes our essence. Not everyone is so inclined of course, and others will take their own true form in other ways, but ultimately it is the mask we wear in order to fit in with society that we must take off in order to be true to ourselves.

Of course, though anglers are floating around with a sense of free spirit, there will always be those among us whose boundaries and beliefs differ from our own. Angling carries with it a bevy of unwritten missives and qualities that we adhere to as a matter of course. Most, if not all, are based upon common sense, which is subjective in itself, and many of the attributes required of an angler are not necessarily clear.

Patience is one such virtue and it is often said that fishermen are blessed with it, but as James O'Gorman noted in *The Practice of Angling* (1845) perhaps patience is not quite so important.

> *Several persons say they have not patience for angling: this is truly ridiculous; we must have patience on all occasions; but I think the word ought to be altogether expunged from the vocabulary of sportsmen, and the word perseverance substituted. If this quality is not inherent in a sportsman, he*

will be a bad hand at either shooting or fishing. How often after many hours of fruitless exertion without success, when all seems blank, may not a fine scull of trout with fins and tail over water, make their appearance, when, if a good angler, you pick up three or four of them in a few minutes, and bless your stars that you persevered to the end!

Perseverance is certainly a handy trait, but neither it nor patience is as valuable as involvement. Becoming an angler does not necessitate the catching of fish, at least not when you are seeking a pastime that is beyond the putting of food on the table.

And while WC Fields' notion that, 'If at first you don't succeed, try, try again. Then quit. No use being a damn fool about it', is perhaps a little blunt, if, after a few days on the bank, the river is not slipping into your dreams then perhaps angling is not for you.

For a novice angler exploring an 'involvement', it is advisable to keep an ear or cast an eye for the local acts of parlance. By adhering to the 'done thing', you are then far more likely to be received by the river and its regulars. Rather like a pool table in a pub, the essence is pretty much the same wherever you drink, but there are always anomalies peculiar to every stream or every bar, and it is far better to be aware of them before you begin a frame.

Fly fishing, and in particular salmon fishing, is far more steeped in tradition and convention than coarse or sea fishing. This is largely due to its development through Victorian culture. British industry was booming during the nineteenth century, and the labour classes found themselves working ever longer hours. For those few who could afford it, the British country-side became a clean and contrasting distraction from the smog of the cities, and interest in country pursuits soared.

Salmon fishing evolved as a pastime for the privileged, and with the railway and road networks spreading deep into the more remote reaches of the British Isles, so wealth and possibility came to areas that had long been wild, unreachable, and from a human perspective at least, deprived.

With growth came rigidity. The Victorian Gentleman was a lover of punctual decorum, and this was soon reflected within the art of fishing itself.

A day on the river would be scheduled, beats and pools allocated and alternated. The angler would never cast his fly upstream but instead across and he would follow it down each pool. Cast and move, allowing any angler working the same bank behind him to cover the water at the same pace as they both work their way downstream.

Should anyone be fishing the far bank then similar courtesies would also be offered. An angler would never move in to fish downstream from another (unless it was a certain distance away) and instead would always begin above him, covering pools the other rod had already fished.

Lunchtime would be at a predetermined hour and any efforts to head back to the river early would be strictly frowned upon, particularly if the intention was made to head for pools not allocated to you.

At the end of the day the ghillie would be handsomely tipped and often any salmon killed offered to the owner of the water before any presumption was made that they might be taken by the captor.

Such traditions have persisted until today, with variances between different rivers and estates in accordance to circumstance or whim. Though the demise of the Atlantic salmon has been felt hard across the north and west, the stronghold of the species in the British Isles, anglers still pay a princely sum to cast for those that remain. To that end the influence of class upon the sport is still very evident, but it would be false to suggest that bankside etiquette is maintained for any gratification or reinforcement of one's own status in society. For many salmon anglers today, adherence to tradition is very much part of their angling identity and enjoyment, particularly if they have cast since childhood - when we are so accepting of rules and authority. To follow similar paths will lead the angler straight back to the mindset of his childhood self, when life was so much more straightforward.

For coarse anglers who do not enjoy both disciplines, the rhetoric of such practices can seem stuffy and unnecessary.

Coarse fishing is not without its own peculiarities though, and these too are largely borne out of respect and consideration for your fellow man.

Some people are less aware than others and I have before had swims spoiled by the actions of other anglers. On one occasion two chaps upstream and on the opposite bank began floating pieces of crust downstream, presumably in the hope of snaring a chub or two.

I was fishing a slack a fair distance from them and I was catching fish too, with a couple of chub and a barbel among dozens of dace, but the bread began to run off a crease in the current and collect in my swim.

The ducks arrived first. Two pairs of mallards who began

chasing the pieces of bread across the surface. That encouraged the local swans to have a beak into the area and soon my swim was unfishable. The birds were sitting in the slack water waiting for the bread to come pacing down the current to them.

I wandered upstream and politely pointed out to the 'chub' fishermen the problems they were causing me, but unfortunately this simply fanned a flame and the stream of bread increased in volume. I could hear the two men giggling away in the bushes above me, and rather than upset myself with a firmer confrontation, I stopped fishing for a time, popped the kettle on and waited until their bread and fun ran out.

Another regular on the river at that time was an angler who never actually seemed to do much fishing, but always seemed to track me down on the banks and tell me of the extraordinary fish he had caught. He was an habitual 'sky-liner' - in that he seemed to have no comprehension that fish in clear water might not take kindly to his presence on the bank.

I could be hunched quietly behind a patch of sedge having gradually built up a near-bank run, and he would suddenly appear right beside me, towering over the water and spooking all the fish. Just in case his sudden manifestation had not caused complete underwater panic, he would then talk in my ear at a hundred decibels.

In case you are wondering, on one occasion I did spot him coming and whispered an appeal as he approached for him to keep low so as to not frighten the chub in my swim.

Initially he obliged - sort of; he bowed for his final few paces. The mention of chub got him excited though and he boomed of his recent success with them on the river and a brace of 7-pounders he had taken. To point out the swim from which he had caught these monsters, he leant out over the water to point downstream. I didn't have another bite.

I seemed to run into this man every time I fished that season, but only once was he fishing himself. On that day I thought I had got the river to myself, and settled into a noted barbel swim with the hope of good sport.

The morning had been slow, but after lunch I took the first of three barbel in an hour and I was set for a dreamy afternoon.

Then he arrived, and of course he opted for the swim immediately above me. I wasn't too concerned at first, happy in the knowledge that the barbel were happily feeding along the crease in front of me, but then he starting fishing.

Having crashed out two leads he proceeded to catapult out some loose feed. Fish pellets were taking the barbel world by storm at the time, and this guy had bought himself a bucket of 'halibut' pellets - baits created to farm feed a flatfish that could grow to hundreds of pounds in weight.

They do make good baits, but are large and packed with protein and oils so a couple are more than enough to fill up an average sized barbel. I should have gently reminded him of this after the first dozen rained into his swim, but chose instead to rely on him possessing some sense. He didn't, and by the time he had fed enough bait to feed every fish in the river, I had gathered my kit and was making my way to another stretch of river.

I told a friend of this incident and he insisted that I should have said something, not least so that I could educate him. But I shy away from confrontation wherever possible and any level of interaction at that moment would just have disturbed my own peace of mind.

That this man was lacking common sense rather than knowingly trying to upset a fellow angler I have no doubt, but in my experience those people who do not display as much awareness as others, and as I mentioned earlier common sense is subjective, are often desperately upset when their actions are questioned.

Sometimes there is less to be gained by questioning another's actions than simply removing yourself from that situation. I had already caught three barbel, and ended up adding four decent chub a few hundred yards upstream. The over-zealous loose-feeder caught nothing (I presume with a fair amount of confidence) but hopefully considered the reason why. If he learned from his mistake then he would have had a successful day . . .

I remember feeling chastened by some of my actions as a young angler, and in some instances I certainly learned the hard way.

It is all too easy for a bored young angler to leave his rod unattended and have a stroll when action is slow, but the first time I did that I returned to find my float sitting in the middle of a lily-bed with the hook fast in a stem.

"Fish must have taken it into the weed . . ." A nearby older angler told me, and from his demeanour I knew at once that he had reeled in my line, taken the bait off and cast it into the pads to make a point. I lost my hook but I understood his sentiment, though perhaps not sufficiently.

A year or two later I was fishing a lake in Eastleigh and doing fairly well. Another angler began chatting to me and I turned round to talk to him. His eyes suddenly widened and his gaze moved behind me and I spun round just in time to see my rod leap off the rests and out into the lake.

It floated, which was a relief, but I had to swim out to retrieve it and that in front of a dozen other anglers who didn't hold back with their laughing and pointing.

Ultimately though, I realised why a rod should never be left unattended, though sometimes it seems others are not so affected by shame. Two lads were fishing with their father on the Kennet and were obviously bored with the whole business. Martin and I had fished past them and were well upstream when one of them came running up to us. They had gone walk-about and one had lost his rod, could Martin, who was wearing chest-waders, come and help?

Martin obliged, and walked back downstream, located the rod and managed to find a safe route out to it. The fish, a barbel, was still attached but stuck in a weed-bed and Martin managed to free it, play the fish out and work his way back to the boys and their father. He didn't even get a thank you, so preoccupied were the lads to photograph and weigh 'their' barbel. It would have been easier to bear if the father had had a word but he too seemed to care little other than for the glory of the capture and Martin lamented later in the evening that he should have unhooked the fish in the water and handed the rod back without a word.

The rise in popularity of certain species or venues certainly seems to coincide with an increase in unethical angling behaviour, and though this could be explained by the simple rise of numbers involved, there does appear to be a proportional imbalance.

This is not surprising when you consider that angling has 'trends' just like any activity. Some anglers will simply follow the herd and fish for the 'in' species at the 'in' locations and it would not be unfair to suggest that if their priorities are so determined then their respect for fellow anglers may be equally superficial.

One positive trend that has grown in recent years is that of fish care. Staples of an angler's kit fifty years ago, such as gaffs and even keepnets, are now frowned upon. Modern carp anglers will unhook their prizes on special mats with a bucket of water nearby to ensure the fish's skin does not dry out. Antiseptic will be applied to any lesions or sores and even the hole in the mouth left by the hook. While such actions may seem hypocritical to some, once a layman accepts that fishing is a basic human need then he will appreciate that the fish, if not being angled for the table are at least being treated with respect and utmost care.

My old friend 'Charles' certainly cared little for the fish he caught. He would always take a keepnet to Swelling Hill, and though I often watched him without success to determine why, he always tipped dead fish back at the end of the day.

Keepnets still have their place in modern angling, but almost exclusively in match fishing. As most matches are five hours or less, then the fish are not going to suffer unduly from their retention, and the majority of fishing matches are carried out with strict rules for the amount and size of fish that may be retained.

Charles' keepnet would, I am certain, not have been wetted again after his family moved him away, though his habit of encroachment is something I have encountered since.

It was yet another trip to the Kennet, this time to a stretch known as Upper Benyons - one of the most well known barbel stretches on the whole river.

Considering it was the first Saturday in September, I was astonished to find the car park empty. There was an England football match on television that evening, but even in the depths of winter there was normally at least one other rod on the river.

The popular swims on the stretch were upstream of the car park, and as a result I normally headed in the opposite direction in order to seek peace among less trodden banks.

With no other anglers there though, I decided to head up to the hotspots and find out what the fuss was all about.

As it turned out, I struggled. The most well fished swim really did look perfect, with a smooth flow, good depth, and a fallen tree which offered a perfect holding spot for fish. I baited towards the tail end of the pool and fished a bait as close to the snags as I dared. Nothing happened.

It made some sense that bites were not forthcoming. Despite the obvious attraction that the swim had for barbel and chub, the fact that they got fished for almost every day of the season would have made them extraordinarily suspicious.

Nevertheless, I quite fancied the challenge of fooling an educated fish and carried on fishing, making subtle changes to the bait and its presentation. By early afternoon, I was still fishless but felt confident that they would feed as the light began to fade.

Another angler and his son came down the bank and looked none too pleased to see me. I offered a smile and a hello but got short shrift in return and they walked past me to a bend below.

A few minutes later the son, who was perhaps ten or eleven, returned.

"Caught anything, mate?" he asked a little sheepishly.

I told him no, a fact I confirmed twice further in the next forty minutes or so when he returned to ask the same question.

After the third reply, I did mention that I was considering heading home to watch the football if sport didn't improve and the boy told me he had wanted to watch the match, but his dad had made him come fishing instead.

Another fifteen minutes ticked by and the boy was back again, this time asking what time I was leaving if I was going to watch the football. It was getting increasingly obvious that his father was sending him up to talk to me and I presumed that was because he fancied my swim. I told the boy that I would probably leave in an hour or two, though in truth I didn't really know what I fancied doing. My decision was soon made much easier.

The man and his son were soon walking up the bank and they had not yet so much as put up a rod.

"If you are off, I'll wait for you to go," the angler said, "don't mind do ya'?"

He then began to unpack his gear, just a couple of yards behind me. He set up two rods, readied rod-rests and all the while was keeping one eye on everything I did.

"You didn't give the bend a go, then?" I asked. I simply couldn't believe that with a couple of miles of river to fish, he was going to sit and wait for the only occupied swim to become available.

He shrugged. "No mate - I like this swim - you don't mind me waiting here, do ya'?"

I did mind, I minded a lot, but felt powerless. He was doing nothing wrong as such, but was certainly pressuring me to leave.

Part of me wanted to stay put until dark just to spite him, but I could take no pleasure in fishing with this chap on my shoulder and wound in to pack up.

His rod-rests were planted in the ground before I had even taken my one out, and both of his baits were cast out before I had finished stowing my rod away.

I said nothing until the son spoke.

"Are you going to watch the football then?"

I could tell he was envious, but before I could answer, his father was speaking over the top of us both.

"He wanted to watch it and I would normally, but it'll be rubbish." He laughed, "I mean - Germany away? We haven't got a chance!"

England had more than one chance, and they scored five of them: 5-1 in Munich and one of the best performances ever by an England side. I was chuffed to have made it home to watch it with friends, and as the fifth goal went in, I cast a thought for the poor lad who was missing it so his dad could fish.

I hope he still makes him feel guilty about it.

Chapter Seven

Afternoon Snooze

Having laid out your rods . . . you are at liberty to smoke,
meditate, read, and even, I think, to sleep.
H.T. SHERINGHAM

After a string of potentially catastrophic incidents, in 2011 the National Transportation Safety Board in the United States called for 'controlled naps' to be incorporated into the shifts of Air Traffic Controllers.

They referred to a study made by NASA in 1995 which determined that a twenty-six-minute nap could improve performance by thirty-four per cent and alertness by fifty-four per cent.

I would imagine that this was a notion received well by both employees and the general public - ultimately, those in air traffic control really do need to keep their minds on the job in hand - but for many people in western culture the nap is something we were encouraged to leave behind in our infant years. It may be true that many cultures practise the siesta, but this is as much about resting when the sun is at its fiercest as it is about enjoying a crafty snooze.

Certainly the overwhelming attitude in Britain is that taking a nap is an unnecessary decadence; a sign of weakness; and as a result we view sleep as a functional need and not a vehicle for pleasure. Closing your eyes for just twenty-six minutes is, to most, something unobtainable. It's all or nothing - seven and a half hours or sod all.

They should take lessons from my father.

I may have resented the comparisons when I was in the midst of pubescent rebellion, but there is no denying that I am my father's son. The gait, the smile and the prominent chin could have come from no one else, but as a teenager you are not in any way middle-aged and out of touch; you are young, misunderstood and immensely cool.

With a settling of hormones comes more reasoned perspective, and the man that to an infant is the only hero in the world once again becomes a person to admire. I feel honoured to be compared to my father today despite the grey hair, though one trait that I have yet to develop myself is his ability to cat-nap.

Both my parents are early risers and enjoy the dawn hours drinking tea and doing puzzles in bed and while both balance this by retiring early of an evening, my father routinely sneaks in an afternoon snooze. No more than twenty minutes, unless he had a third pint at lunchtime, and occasionally as few as ten, but always post-lunch and always in whatever circumstance he finds himself.

He might announce it if in company, and then seems to simply flick a switch and doze before waking refreshed and rejuvenated. I have tried on occasion to replicate his ability, but always end up in deep sleep which takes me too far away from the day and leaves me groggy and confused afterwards.

Even the discomfort of a riverbank does not restrict him. Because he doesn't fall too far into the unconscious, he can hold his body in relatively awkward positions. He is relaxed but rigid

- eyes open long before he ever topples.

It is here, on the bank, that I come closest to matching his ability. Too often I've had forty or even eighty winks on a sunny afternoon, but once or twice I've taken twenty and been the better for it. The reason for this is purely my state of mind. Fishing is, after all, the ultimate meditation.

My wife Sue practises meditation on a daily basis; initially as a device to combat illness, but now very much as a method of relaxation and enjoyment. She will sometimes seem tired and harangued but after a half hour alone will return with a dreamy smile and a sense of perspective.

She was quick to identify the effect that fishing had on my own mind and the similarities with her own experiences.

"What do I think about when fishing?" she once asked. To which I shrugged and answered, "Everything and nothing . . ."

When stresses of work or finance are too great to leave at home, the riverbank is a perfect place to digest them. Withdrawing oneself from the source of anxiety gives an incredibly balanced perspective of it. Taking a step back is not always easy or obvious but it undoubtedly works, and once rationality supersedes our tendency to wallow in distress and self-pity, we become that much more receptive to those things that are really important.

We are not simply putting things off until tomorrow, though that in itself is no bad thing. Instead we are rationalising and prioritising, weeding out the troublesome little thoughts that nag our minds and yet have no real bearing upon us.

In order to fish successfully, be that by catching fish or simply being, we have to first empty our minds of the dross. Then, when we are focusing on the matter in hand, the rod, the reel, the way the water moves, the choice of fly or size of hook, then we are moving away from that initial burden of pressure from our other reality. This is reality. Flicking a piece of bread on to the nose of that chub under the willow. Landing the line without a splash and getting a rise from a wild brown trout.

With everything in its right place, our minds then drift with the current. Casting is effortless, Zen-like. We are tuned in and yet utterly tuned out. Relying on instinct and trusting to natural ability and reaction. At this point we are not thinking of work or credit card bills and we have long stopped thinking about the process of fishing. We are merely being and though it sounds a hollow existence, it is the very best place for us to be.

This is what I meant when I told Sue, 'everything and nothing' - and this is what she could immediately identify as a state of meditation. A place where she was training her own mind to find.

And in such a place, detached so deliciously from self created reality, we owe ourselves a moment to reel in, pull down the brim of our hat, feel the sun on our skin and snooze. After all, the fish, at this point in the day, are very much likely to be doing the same thing.

Walden Pond near Concord in Massachusetts is in reality as unlikely looking a 'pond' as we might imagine. This is not some intimate, lily-strewn nursery pool like Swelling Hill, where young lads cut their angling teeth against half-pound tench and four-inch rudd.

Instead, Walden is a 60-acre, 100-foot deep kettle hole formed by retreating glaciers over ten thousand years ago. It holds fish, and according to Henry David Thoreau, Walden's most devout champion, it supports many.

Thoreau was a leading proponent of nineteenth century western philosophy, and a key member of the Transcendentalist movement of the 1840s and 1850s. The transcendentalists believed that people were too easily corrupted by the constraints of modern culture and society; that Man was at his best and most pure when self-reliant and independent.

In order to explore his own self and expand his spirituality and self-reliance, Thoreau spent two years living in a small cabin amidst the wooded banks of Walden Pond. Here he wrote his 1854 work *Walden or Life in the Woods* which has remained his most familiar work since his death from tuberculosis at the age of just 44.

The pond itself was a key part of Thoreau's life in the woods, providing him, foremost, with a source of clean water but also as a muse for his words and a source of food. Though his fishing would more likely have been driven by a need to eat, it is clear from his writing that he gained a far deeper pleasure from angling than could be attained by simply sating his hunger.

At length you slowly raise, pulling hand over hand, some horned pout squeaking and squirming to the upper air. It was very queer, especially in dark nights, when your thoughts had wandered to vast and cosmogonal themes in other spheres, to feel this faint jerk, which came to interrupt your dreams and link you to Nature again. It seemed as if I might next cast my line upward into the air, as well as downward into this element, which was scarcely more dense. Thus I caught two fishes as it were with one hook.

Thoreau seemed particularly in awe of the pickerel in Walden and he mentions fish in excess of seven pounds being taken. Though it is likely that there were pickerel far larger than this in such a large water Thoreau does not mention them and from his descriptions of the water itself he surely would have seen them.

Such was the clarity in the lake that Thoreau could see the bottom at impressive depth. One winter, when ice-fishing, he lost his axe through a hole he had previously made but could still see it on the bottom at least twenty-five feet down. He managed to retrieve it with a slip noose tied to the end of the 'longest piece of birch' he could find.

The water clarity gave him good views of perch, fish he felt reached over two pounds in weight and seemed to be charmed by music. Thoreau would spend many evenings sitting on his boat playing his flute and remarked that the perch seemed to float around him as if in response to his melodies.

The waters of Walden formed physical sustenance for Thoreau throughout his life in the woods, but an arguably greater affectation was that which he found in his personal journey. The pond became symbolic of his own self, and the condition of the water and the life within it seemed to echo his mood and direction. The water of Walden had seeped into his veins as a child and now in adulthood he was able to quantify its influence.

I have spent many an hour, when I was younger, floating over its surface as the zephyr willed, having paddled my boat to the middle, and lying on my back across the seats, in a summer forenoon, dreaming awake, until I was aroused by the boat touching the sand, and I arose to see what shore my fates had impelled me to; days when idleness was the most attractive and productive industry. Many a forenoon have I stolen away, preferring to spend thus the most valued part of the day; for I was rich, if not in money, in sunny hours and summer days, and spent them lavishly.

As I always argue to those people who question the value of angling, if you could spend a lazy afternoon beside a beautiful, glistening river would you not? And they answer, always, that of course they would. And I say to them, well imagine having an excuse for being there - that is fishing.

Thoreau was captured by the very water itself and allowed himself to be utterly seduced by it. His childhood self, floating on the breeze upon Walden, enjoyed a state of mind that people in modern society either strive desperately to find as a therapy for the stresses of life, or avoid touching for fear of that reality discounting the value of their daily grind.

Thoreau was rediscovering his youth when he chose to live his life of simplicity and austerity and by doing so was lifting the veil that adulthood had laid upon all whimsical thought and belief. We complain habitually of the weather and recall the long, hot summers of childhood when days were endless, warm and hazy yet in reality those summers were no different to those of today, we were simply more receptive as children. We existed in the moment, with no care for what was happening tomorrow or what we would eat for dinner, or how the hell we were going to pay the council tax bill.

With lunch eaten and a few fish caught, we anglers are heading back to that simple life. Time is just a pain-in-the

-arse dimension that dictates our movements within our other lives. Here and now is all about this very moment. The slightest dip of the float, the song of a blackcap, the shape of the stream. If we were to close our eyes now, just for a few moments, then we wouldn't sleep but would drift briefly into a dream; just long enough to sharpen our senses yet slow our heart rate. Become even closer to the water.

Probably best to reel the line in . . .

My friend Martin has a remarkable ability to sleep-fish. As I mentioned earlier, he doesn't drive and so when opportunities to fish do present themselves, he likes to make the most of them.

A few seasons back he put in a series of two or three day sessions on the Kennet, relying on trains and lifts to get him to and from the water and then tucking himself into the long grass away from the world.

I joined him for the second night of one of his stays and found him buoyed by his success of the previous evening. He had taken four barbel through the dark hours and each one he had hooked while asleep. Martin wasn't using bite alarms to alert him to a bite, but instead was dozing with the rod in his hand and a loop of line tucked over his finger.

He would get comfortable on his chair and let his mind drift while still maintaining limited control of his body. When a bite came his reaction would be conscious but from within his subconscious. He would not jerk awake with any disorientation, but would lift into the bite and respond to that first lunge while easing his mind back into full awareness.

I tried the technique for myself, getting comfortable and lowering a piece of bacon grill into a hole under the near bank.

In time, I felt that heaviness in my eyes and instead of blinking myself awake let the feeling slide while allowing some focus to remain on my right hand which held the butt of the rod and the feel of the line across my index finger. I drifted.

When I woke, it wasn't in composed response to a lunging fish but with the echo of a belly laugh resounding through my head. Martin had stirred, glanced across to me and was now falling about. I had successfully fallen asleep but where I had leant backwards as I dozed so my rigid right arm had pivoted, lifting the rod tip directly above me and swinging the bait out of the water and around my ankles.

Martin calmed eventually and I tried the trick again, but with exactly the same result and while I was never going to catch anything without a bait in the water, I very much doubt any fish were hanging around with the volume of Martin's cackles.

Though my night-time dozing technique went back to the drawing board I have managed to hone my daytime snoozing, though its depth is very much dependent upon the season.

In summer, especially early season when the days are long and the sun high, the afternoon lull seems to affect the angler and fish alike. A whole day beside the water can be over eighteen hours and nothing will stay alert for all of that time.

Opening day is the classic day when an afternoon nap becomes a near necessity. Having slept little if at all, those first few hours are charged with adrenaline; the excitement of a new day and a new season adding a surreal edge to those routines that remain familiar but are less intuitive after a three month break.

It is inevitable that the momentum of the day will dip and it will almost certainly happen as the fish shy away from the afternoon sun. The water temperature will have risen and the sheer amount of light breaking through the surface layers will coax the fish into a response. They may sunbathe or tuck up safe in a weed-bed, if it is very early in the season then they might start chasing one another in carnal distraction, but whatever their reaction to the conditions, it is likely to lead to fewer bites.

On the bank you are feeling pleasantly numbed by the soporific mood that has descended, and not only is sleep a natural progression of mind at this point, it will also give you greater edge for the evening - when the fish start to move again and the intensity returns.

It is on a long day such as this when my inability to catnap like my father is not too much of a hindrance. A two-hour dive into a proper sleep cycle will not eat up too much of the day. Having said that, there have been times when sleep has eaten up almost the whole day and yet I have still been rewarded for it. When stresses of the week have been so great, the sudden wallop of relaxation you find in that other place is like taking a dozen Temazepam.

I arrived beside the river on one July morning and wandered a mile or so downstream out of sight of any other angler. That week had been particularly draining and far too many of my workplace plights were working deep into my dreams. Having lain down my gear, I sat on a small tussock for a moment watching the river crease beneath me. Within seconds my shoulders slumped and my jaw almost hit the floor. I hit the proverbial wall and had nothing with which to climb it.

As I closed my eyes the sound of the river came like the caress of a hand. Not a trickle or splash, but a gentle and constant kiss of liquid air. I was gone and deeply asleep within moments and would have stayed there far longer had the ants not found me.

I felt groggy when I woke and a fair few ants had had a nibble before they roused me. It was well into the afternoon, and despite having not even unbagged a rod, decided on a walk upstream. I headed to the top of the stretch, the other side of the crowds, figuring that the walk would get my circulation going and perk me up a bit. The sun was high and hot and I found shade beneath a horse chestnut where the grass was thick and lush and felt like a soft, cool pillow . . .

This time I slept for longer but woke feeling so much more refreshed and also a little chilly. The sun had caught my skin as I lay near the ant nest and now it was beginning to dip, the cool air prickled me with a shiver. I had less than half an hour of the day left and had still not wetted a line. I was tempted to make my way home, but felt compelled to make one cast from where I sat. In fact I had three, and each time the line had tightened and a fat chub had come to the net. A brace and a half of chub all approaching five pounds was a good day's fishing and I had only fished for twenty minutes. As I drove home I pondered whether I would have caught at all had I not given into that first overwhelming need for sleep. I probably could have fought against it, but then, adrenalised, I would most likely have fished without proper thought. And certainly I would not have found myself in the grass pillow swim casting single baits and finding chub so willing to take them. Though it might seem fanciful to suggest that the river was rewarding me for listening to my body and resting my mind rather than focusing it upon the fish, it is more than likely that my benign presence in that swim meant that those chub felt safe in the water beside me.

With a lazy, almost token cast I thrice put a bait among them without causing any alarm.

Most importantly that day, though, was the contentment I felt on the journey home. I had arrived at the river in top gear with my foot to the floor and in a state of mind where if I didn't catch and catch quickly then the pressure would have affected me. Instead, sleep had taken me gently down through the gears to the point where actually catching a fish was of secondary importance to just being and in that state I could not fail.

As a sleepless child I would try and relax by imagining myself drifting through space. I would be comfortable - in fact my bed would be in a small unpowered bubble in which I was quite safe as I drifted through the darkness. My destination was irrelevant, as was my purpose, all that mattered was floating easily among the stars where I could breathe gently and deeply and drift . . .

Henry Thoreau would have had the same sensation as the breeze nudged his boat across Walden pond. Laying down with his eyes on the sky, warmed by the sun and breathing that crisp cool air that sits above any water's surface. The power of water as a tool with which to unlock our subconscious is evident whatever its form. My wife Sue loves to sit beside the sea and just absorb its being. She could spend days there, not sunbathing, not fishing, not doing anything other than feeling and being.

The alternative title for *The Compleat Angler* is 'The Contemplative Man's Recreation', and it is this part of the day when Izaak Walton's secondary title seems most authentic. Later on in the day, when the world once again stirs with intent, our focus will be centred upon our float tops, but for know we can relax and breathe.

If we do doze, then perhaps we should learn Martin's night fishing technique. It is possible and I managed it a couple of winters back, though that was in the afternoon.

Feeling the sun on your face on a late January day is not just a pleasure but a reassurance. After the dark days around the solstice, there is again some warmth in the rays even if the air temperature is colder.

I had popped to the river knowing that I would be alone and so it proved. The water temperature was desperately low. So low that had I bothered dipping the thermometer I probably would have headed straight home, but the river was also just spilling over its banks and that would mean the fish might be easier to find.

A favourite spot in such conditions was just off the edge of a weir sill, where a gentle back eddy formed a deep, almost static hole. It always felt odd lowering in a bait with a single swan shot for weight just inches from the torrent of the main weir, but for the most part, save the odd larger branch crashing through, it would remain there undisturbed.

I had travelled light with just a rod, net and bottle of water and a few bits of bait and tackle in my coat pockets. I had toyed with bringing a chair, knowing I was likely to be sedentary for long periods, but with a fairly solid ground beneath my feet thought I could do without.

I propped myself up against a fencepost and wriggled into a comfortable position just as the sun broke through the cloud.

I hadn't been cold up to that point, but I now felt warm and within minutes I was feeling drowsy. It is a lovely sensation when on the brink of sleep to cast a thought around your body and find that every part of you is cosy and secure. No toes needed tucking in and no draft was tickling its way inside a sleeve or exposed flank.

I let my thoughts focus upon my hands. I knew I was going to doze, but felt confident I could do so while keeping a safe grip on the rod. I took a loop of line with my left hand and let it sit quite tightly around two fingers. I was wearing gloves but knew a bite from a barbel would be positive enough to penetrate the wool. I rested the rod itself between my crossed feet and then tucked the butt into my side with my right hand holding a loose grip. Nothing would snatch the rod now without me stopping it - time to let myself drift.

I imagined the bait on the bottom, fairly still but nudging occasionally as an extra few gallons of water thundered past. There would be barbel nearby, maybe under the sill itself where the back current would have bored out the gravel. Surely one would find the bait . . .

I was asleep when I felt the first pluck, and didn't raise myself fully from the subconscious. The line had flickered and trembled a few times in the spray from the deluge and had tightened too as a lump of weed rolled through the swim. This had felt different though, more deliberate. Definitely fishy - though it could have been a line bite or a gudgeon with an appetite. Nothing more though, so I let myself drift back down.

The bite, the strike and my waking all happened within a moment but there was no panic, I simply found myself standing up and bending into a heavy fish. The line had tweaked again, rousing me slightly once more, before firmly tightening and the process had felt as natural as if I had been fully awake.

It was clearly a barbel, no other fish would have such solid strength, and it seemed intent on sitting tight to the bottom under the sill using the weight of the water to resist my pressure.

The line was being buffeted by the main overflow and I worried that it might rattle the hook free. I pointed the rod tip straight down and under the surface and this time let the weight of the water work for me. The fish gradually ceded ground as the power of the flow against the line inched it towards open water.

Then it woke up, kicked and surged out in front of me, taking a few turns of line but also kiting slightly to the right where the water was deep but quieter. I knew then that with patience I would have my prize and so it proved.

It was a bulky fish, with small fins and a relatively small head but in absolutely prime condition. I do not believe that that fish could have weighed any more than it did that day and at 13lb 9oz was actually half an inch shorter than an 8-pounder I had taken in the same pool a fortnight before.

Not that it mattered or I really cared, for I was glowing warm on a cold day and would take that sense and float on it all the way home.

Chapter Eight

Tea-time

*There are few hours in life more agreeable than
the hour dedicated to the ceremony known as afternoon tea*
HENRY JAMES, THE PORTRAIT OF A LADY

Charles I had a particularly turbulent reign. Tiffs with the Church, the Spanish, the Irish and ultimately his own Parliament, and then to top it off having his head lopped off in 1649.

He was a man of great dignity and was said to have worn warm clothing on the day of his execution so that no one might mistake a shiver for fear. Oliver Cromwell, who usurped Charles after the Civil War, clearly respected the man he had overthrown as he allowed the head to be sewn back on to the body in order to allow Charles' family to pay their respects and bury him whole.

Perhaps if Charles could have rallied enough support to survive for a few more years, then his reign may not have ended at the hands of the New Model Army, for it is widely accepted that during the late 1650s the greatest British panacea of them all was making its mark.

Tea.

The celebrated diarist Samuel Pepys makes reference to his

first taste of tea in his entry dated September 25th, 1660:

> *To the office, where Sir W. Batten, Coll. Slingsby, and I sat*
> *a while; and Sir R. Ford coming to us about some business,*
> *we talked together of the interest of this kingdom to have a*
> *peace with Spain and a war with France and Holland -*
> *where Sir R. Ford talked like a man of great reason and*
> *experience. And afterwards did send for a Cupp of Tee (a*
> *China drink of which I never had drank before) and went*
> *away.*

And that is about as enthused as Pepys got from his experience, though he was a man famous for his indulgences in whatever seventeenth century London life could offer him so perhaps the subtleties of tea were slightly lost.

Nevertheless, the very fact that Pepys was a man with a penchant for contemporary living does suggest that tea in 1660 was a very modern drink. The leaves that Pepys tasted would have originated in China, where people had been wise to the tea-plant's properties for a couple of millennia. Legend has it that it was in 2737 BC that the Emperor Shen Nung was about to sip of freshly boiled water when the breeze blew some leaves from a nearby bush into his bowl.

Europeans began importing tea in the seventeenth century, and following the recently restored Charles II marriage to Catherine of Braganza the drink became fashionable in the royal court.

Catherine had enjoyed tea in her native Portugal and being in such a position of influence her habit was soon shared by her new subjects.

It was something of an insignificance at the time, the Restoration of the Monarchy overshadowing pretty much anything else that year, but Charles I could never have supposed as he knelt before the block that not only would his own son Charles return as King to the throne of England, but that his daughter-in-law would have such an influence upon future British culture.

The arrival of tea also puts into perspective the writings of Izaak Walton who would have completed the first edition of *The Compleat Angler* without even knowing tea existed. How did he cope? He must have felt something was missing from his day.

According to the UK Tea Council, over 60 billion cups of tea are consumed in Britain every year, equating to 165 million cups per day. Not too many of those are drunk on the riverbank, but those that are will almost certainly be the most well received.

Many anglers owe a debt of gratitude to Sir James Dewar, inventor in 1892 of the vacuum flask. Tea or coffee can be made up in the morning and then drunk at any given point during the day. Flasks are convenient and reasonably economic, but do have their failings. Glass flasks are obviously prone to breaking and though some modern hard plastics are tough enough to comfortably last a whole season, their delivery of tea can be a disappointment.

Tea tastes best when it is almost too hot to drink and when it has been made from boiling water (not boiled - the leaves need to properly scold in order to release all their flavour - and water should never be re-boiled either, this reduces the oxygen content which in turn affects the flavour). The only way to achieve this on the riverbank is by boiling a kettle there and then, but this in turn brings its own problems.

A thermos can slip into a pocket or landing-net and be of little encumbrance when travelling light and roving. It might not deliver the same taste but is less of a burden than taking a kettle, fuel, water and milk as separate components. The issue of taste is something many anglers take rather seriously, though. If you are going to take a canister of liquid that is going to leave you even mildly dissatisfied, then it may as well be water or instant coffee. On the other hand, if you value a cup of tea as part of your fishing experience then tea-making equipment becomes as essential as a rod or reel.

Some anglers, particularly those after carp or fishing for a period of days, will have a stove as part of their kit. Most likely gas-powered, they will inevitably include a kettle along with pans used for cooking food on the bank. Carrying half a kitchen to a swim is only really worth it when you are staying there for longer than a day of course, and many anglers doing so will make use of wheelbarrows or pack-horses to ease the load.

For many years I made use of a Trangia. These are ingeniously designed little stoves originating from Sweden and designed for camping. They consist of a variety of different sized aluminium pots (and kettle) which fit inside one another like russian dolls, making a light and compact package.

Fuel (normally methylated spirit) is poured into the small brass burner which produces a surprisingly efficient heat. When camping, I have cooked a variety of meals with the Trangia including multi-element dishes and risottos which have tasted absolutely fine. The kettle takes a little while to boil and doesn't hold an awful lot of water, but delivers hot drinks with little fuss.

On the flipside however, is the fact that you have to take all the components with you when more often than not you only need the burner and kettle. Separating the pieces is unwise as they will inevitably end up behind the washing machine or tucked under the spare tyre, and the whole bundle does not fit together properly when incomplete.

Added to that is the fuel issue. Meths, as any self-respecting tramp will tell you, has its uses but is not a pleasant substance. The smell gets everywhere, and happily permeates the plastic bottle in which it lives. Fish are far more sensitive to smells and chemicals than we are, and too often after a biteless day after chub I have noticed my cheese-paste smelling even less pleasant than usual. Methylated spirits are designed to be foul tasting in order to discourage human consumption, so it is no wonder they might be off-putting to a fish.

Another problem with the Trangia is the wind. An alcohol flame burns with little colour and no smoke and a sly gust of wind can snuff it out with a whisper leaving the fuel to evaporate and the kettle cold.

Despite this, I happily made do with my stove until one Christmas when my parents presented me with a Kelly kettle. Frankly, it changed my life.

I had seen pictures of 'Storm' kettles in the past but had never used one and had no idea just how simple and effective they are.

The design is similar to that of a samovar, a pot used extensively in Russia and other parts of Eastern Europe and the Middle-East. A heat source, traditionally coal or charcoal, is used to boil water which itself is housed around the 'chimney' of the device. They were built to extravagant designs and may date back as far as 3500 years.

The Kelly kettle is more robust and functional and was developed in Ireland at the start of the twentieth century utilising heat-conductive metals such as aluminium and steel.

The concept is simple. A fire is started in the round detachable base and the water-jacket placed on top. The jacket is cylindrical and hollow, tapering to a narrow outlet at the top. The design creates an impressive draw, particularly in cold weather, with the energy produced by the fire travelling upwards and heating the water in the jacket surround. The water can boil in as little as three minutes.

The base also has a couple of round ventilation holes which can be faced into the wind, creating maximum draw for the fire.

They do burn fuel quickly, and it is always wise to gather a selection of twigs before lighting which are then fed into the outlet at the top.

Since I stopped smoking, I have to remind myself to take a lighter or a box of matches when I go fishing, but otherwise all the fuel required can be found on the bank.

Newspaper can make the initial blaze somewhat easier to form, though in recent years I take a small bundle of whittles that I carve in order to light our fire at home and they burn far better than paper. Dead elder is probably the best wood to find on the bankside, but equally good, and often abundant, are the dead and dry stalks of cow-parsley, hogweed, nettles and reeds which are often within reach of the kettle itself. Just this winter I challenged myself to boil the kettle without getting up from my fishing chair - an achievement, I decided, that would be rewarded by the capture of a perch. It wasn't easy, and I had to stretch for the last few dead nettles, but I was triumphant and my prize came almost as soon as I drained the last mouthful of tea.

What the Kelly gives above all though, is ritual.

Anticipation is so often as important as the event itself, and just as we feel so stimulated by the road to the river, so the process of boiling a kettle can give so much more than just a cracking cup of tea.

When I smoked I would roll my own and the process of taking tobacco, gossamer-thin paper and a filter-tip and creating a neat little cylinder was as satisfying as burning the thing.

Occasionally today I see a friend about to roll and find myself interrupting them and doing the job for them. Afterwards I always feel a tinge of guilt for having deprived them of part of their experience, though I never think to ask if the taste has been affected by adjustment of process.

Similarly, such is the pleasure in lighting and burning a Kelly kettle, that I have found myself bickering on the bank over sparking rights. Chris will often want to make the first cup, but might get too sidetracked by perch to get on with the job in hand. If it is his turn to bring the kettle, and I have been beside the river for any period of time before him, then my needs for a drink can prompt a spiky situation. Fortunately though, when the tea is made then we are both winners and the spikiness is only evident after the inevitable dip of a float produces a perch. As I mentioned at lunchtime, every angler knows that a fish will bite the moment you reach for a mug.

Tea and angling is not a new marriage, though it is relatively modern. Izaak Walton may have angled in a time before tea, but that great writer H.T. Sheringham makes reference to its importance in his book *Trout Fishing*:

The evening in fishing begins, to my mind, as nearly as possible at five o'clock. The interval between afternoon and evening is bridged by tea, that modest stimulant which is so refreshing to mind and body after a hot, tiring, and possibly unproductive day. Nearly all my friends laugh at my enthusiasm for tea, but I do not mind how much they laugh so long as they do not interfere with my plans for ensuring it. And I have converted a man here and there to my way of thinking, for which I do not always get thanked. There is nobody so desolate as the person accustomed to afternoon tea when for any reason that luxury is not obtainable. The angler who has grown to be accustomed to it would be well advised to take some trouble to get it. The provision of tea sometimes seems a new and rather revolutionary idea to dames who inhabit riverside cottages, but after coquetting with it awhile they usually come to see that it is not one of the impossibilities, and presently you will find that they take quite kindly to the business. Failing the convenient cottage or handy inn, there is of late years the new resource of the vacuum flask, so nobody now need despair of tea at the proper time.

Sheringham's mention of the vacuum flask came with a rather sombre portent. These words were written around 1915, and in the ensuing years so many families found themselves ripped apart by the Great War. Many of the handy inns and convenient cottages would sadly vanish with either a lack of proprietors or of people to patronise them - both lost in the trenches of France and Belgium.

Though it is impossible to gauge just what sort of impact war may have had on the angler's relationship with tea, sales of the flask would certainly have benefitted. Today, nearly a century on, our culture of convenience has long left the tea-room as a relic of the past. Small cafés still struggle on, but battle now against the American inspired coffee-shop juggernauts. Fashion takes us into Costa or Starbucks to sip a Skinny Latte while talking loudly about marketing plans and brand image. It is all too clinical. Disposable cups and plastic spoons.

Don't get me wrong, I like coffee and have friends who will tuck a cafetière into their fishing bag, but what seems sad is that we feel the need to take a drink on the run. Morning commuters pace the platforms with a plastic cup in hand; the contents cannot be appreciated - at least they cannot be savoured - but without that hot curl of plastic sitting in a cardboard pot they would feel too detached from the essential routine that precedes a working day.

To actually stop and sit and enjoy a hot drink with the ritual and process that precedes it, is something that we should give more time to and at least anglers have the opportunity to do exactly that.

If you have the time, and unless the fish have you completely distracted then there is *always* time, then tea-time is a perfect chance to stop, reflect and enjoy. It is even better if your cup of tea comes with a slice of the best cake ever made.

I do not have a sweet tooth in 'normal' life but my angling self is rather partial to a biscuit or a slab of something fruit-filled. Shortbread is always worth keeping in your tackle bag being fairly cheap, keeping for months and full of buttery loveliness.

Though keen as a child (chocolate chip cookies were my forté)

I no longer bake myself, and though there are some fine shop-bought cakes to be found, the very best bankside treats are homemade.

A dozen of us fished on the Kennet in celebration of my father's seventy-fifth birthday and the highlight was definitely tea-time when my mum arrived with tins of fresh goodies.

More recently I stayed at my sister's while spending a couple of days on the same river and on the morning of the second day, which just happened to be my birthday, I was presented with a stunning fruitcake, complete with candles, that I ate far too much of that afternoon.

Fruitcake is always a favourite and I did know one shop that sold a particularly good home-made one. They were not cheap, but Opening Day a few seasons back was good enough excuse to pick one up.

I was fishing with Chris, Hugh and Trevor, and we had two acres of prime crucian carp water to ourselves. The pond was an hour and a half from home but still I made it just as the sun was rising. Hugh was already fishing, but had yet to have a bite. In fairness he had set up at the shallower end of the lake where he could be sociable (it was Opening Day) and where the fish would head as the sun warmed the water.

I didn't want to wait too long for any interest and settled into a swim on the opposite bank where the sun was already kissing the surface.

By the time Chris and Trev had arrived, I had two or three fish bubbling before me and just as Chris crept up for a chat my float slipped away. It was a tench, rather appropriate for the first fish of the season, but fish were still active next to the lily-pads and my next cast, with Chris still beside me, saw a delicate dip on the float and a golden bulge as I struck into a crucian.

The lake only held around 150 crucians but the majority were of specimen size and this first fish was typical of the stock. It weighed 2lb 9oz and was soon followed by another 2-pounder and one just an ounce off the mark.

Trev had set up diagonally opposite me and was soon into fish himself. His method was fascinating and had been honed from his years as an unashamed roach fanatic. He had dried bread in an airing cupboard until it turned into weightless cardboard which when rehydrated took on the consistency of blancmange. This bread pudding was then moulded around a piece of bread-flake on a size 12 hook and lowered in.

The blancmange would break down in the water leaving a neat pile of milky mush with Trev's hookbait in the middle. The crucians certainly approved.

My own bait was a fiendish concoction, the contents of which I was coy over. Trev later suggested he detected tutti-fruity pop-up lager oil with rosehip essence and owl tears, but in truth it was basically cat biscuit paste. I was enjoying some incredible sport with it though, and by the time the clank of kettles rang out to indicate morning tea I had taken eight crucians to nearly three pounds.

I was excited to share my fruitcake as we sipped our tea but though Trev and Chris seemed keen, Hugh was less so. He had a few crumbs but said he would save himself for the cake his wife Sue had made in honour of the day.

I could only imagine that Hugh was not a fan of fruit because this cake looked as good as it tasted. What I hadn't appreciated though was the fact that his wife Sue is one of the finest bakers in the world.

We carried on taking crucians though sport slowed with the sun at its highest. At mid-afternoon Hugh retired to his van for a snooze, returning refreshed and with a cake tin in hand.

The kettles were fired up once more and we gathered again for refuelling.

The cake was a sponge. Impossibly bouncy and moist, with a dusting of sugar and a perfect colour. The outside was lightly browned and sweetened with a touch of caramelisation while in the middle was a thin layer of butter-cream and the best (home-made) plum jam I have tasted.

Even Hugh was taken aback and he knew what was coming. Chris, Trev and I simply lost ourselves in utter indulgence.

We had a second and third cup of tea and a second slice of cake, and when Hugh nodded and said it was the best cake Sue had ever made, we all argued that it was the best cake anyone had ever made. No wonder Hugh had been reluctant to tarnish his day with a lump of my fruitcake.

We fished on, and caught plenty more, with the best fish coming as it was almost too dark to see. It fell to Hugh and weighed 3lb 7oz and was a fitting end to a perfect Opening Day.

The swim beside our tea and cake spot was subsequently christened 'Sue's swim' such was the impact of her creation and was a productive spot that season even if it has not witnessed quite such a perfect afternoon tea since.

Tea has been particularly associated with the afternoon since the 1840s when Anna Russell, then Duchess of Bedford, found herself hungry at four in the afternoon and called for a cup of tea and some bread and butter. Dinner was traditionally taken well into the evening, and with luncheon a fairly light affair a long gap would sit between meals. Anna enjoyed her impromptu snack and it became a regular habit, in time incorporating cakes and sandwiches and becoming a social occasion that formed a fixture right across the middle and upper classes.

Today, we take tea with far less rigidity; a necessity if we are to drink 165 million cups a day. A cup of tea is viewed as a thing of comfort, and in the world of television soaps an un-rivalled remedy for anything.

"Oh dear, my whole family has been brutally murdered . . ."

"Never mind, love - I'll put the kettle on . . ."

I shouldn't scoff. Tea does have proven benefits to health and contains phenolic compounds that research suggests help reduce the risk of cancer. Tea can also contain brandy as I discovered one New Year's Day on Dartmoor. We were blowing the cob-webs away after an especially late evening and my head was particularly sore after my brother-in-law Mark had pro-duced a bottle of 'Dogfish Head Stout' at around five that very morning. Touted as the strongest beer in the world, the Dogfish was pretty much undrinkable, but we still drank it and at well over twenty per cent alcohol it was a nightcap too far even on New Year's Eve.

A stomp around a couple of tors in a howling wind had done much for our heads but we were jaded and needed a pick-me-up before we made for home. Remarkably, given that we were seemingly the only people daft enough to be on Dartmoor in such weather, we found an open snack van in one of the car parks. Amusingly named 'The Hound of the Basket-Meals', our hero had tea and coffee ready to go and after he took our money he reached a couple of bottles from under the counter.

"I'd recommend brandy for the tea and whisky for the coffee . . ." he smiled.

We didn't argue, and boy did it taste good. I got a second cup too from my wife the designated driver.

Alcohol is unlikely to feature in many anglers' mugs though a bankside drink can offer as much relief as our Dartmoor infusions.

Martin and I had spent the winter chasing a shoal of chub on one of the canalised sections of the river Kennet. It was a small shoal but with a good average size and though we had not caught vast amounts of fish, the smallest had still nudged the five pound mark.

We had either not seen the weather forecast or had not heeded it, for by the time we arrived at the river the wind was blowing hard and the sky darkening. As we walked along the bank the snow started falling and we thought it best to get the brollies up in the hot swim and wait for the worst of the weather to pass before actually fishing.

The weather worsened, and we focused further on keeping ourselves out of it. We overlapped our umbrellas and pinned them down with guy ropes, using a piece of tarpaulin to cover the gap between them and cocoon ourselves and our gear into relative warmth.

With no let up in the weather we decided to set up a single rod and take it in turns to fish, the non-angler being in control of the Trangia which thankfully I had brought.

In the lee of the brollies the Trangia fired up quite easily and our relay began, though tea duty was far more pleasurable than fishing.

Feeling for bites in a sub-zero windchill was a cruel game, but hot mugs kept our fingers frostbite free and we began to enjoy the spirit of the day.

Part of our primeval instinct is to simply survive and in adverse conditions to be safe is a reassuring pleasure. Sheltering from an unexpected rainstorm can be particularly satisfying, not least because you enjoy stolen moments.

Sue and I were walking while on honeymoon in Dorset and we could see a thundery squall that was going to wallop us amidships. A hundred yards ahead of us was a large gnarled yew tree and just as we reached it the first drops of rain began to hit us.

The tree created the most perfect shelter though, with a couple of larger roots curving up into the trunk to form perfect seats. The needles above us were so thick that nothing was getting through and yet it was quite a fantastic little storm. Our feet (mine in flip-flops) were dry and yet inches away from our toes rushed a river where minutes before was a path.

After a few minutes we stopped looking for signs of the weather easing and instead were totally absorbed within the moment. We were warm, dry and in that place at that moment time was wholly irrelevant. We would go nowhere until the rain stopped, and the weather was our law not the ticking hand of a clock.

Back on the Kennet, thoughts of chub had all but dissolved into the snow. The cheese-paste bait had remained untouched yet we were utterly content. Facing adversity (though let's face it, we were hardly attacking the north ridge of Everest) often brings out a twisted sense of humour and we were laughing well.

The wind was pounding, the snow and hail unrelenting and

at some point we would have to get absolutely soaking wet in order to pack up and go home.

Had we had enough tea-bags and permission to do so then we would have happily sat it out all night and maybe nick a chub before we left but as it was we were happy to huddle on our chairs and drink the best tea ever brewed.

Chapter Nine

Serious Fishing

You did not kill the fish only to keep alive and to sell for food, he thought. You killed him for pride and because you are a fisherman. You loved him when he was alive and you loved him after. If you love him, it is not a sin to kill him. Or is it more?

ERNEST HEMINGWAY, THE OLD MAN AND THE SEA

The smallmouth bass is one of the most sought after fish in the United States. Bass fishing is big business with professional anglers earning literally millions of dollars in prize money and sponsorship.

Native to the Mississippi and St Lawrence rivers the small-mouth prospered in distribution after the development of the railway networks in the nineteenth century. They are a hardy species tolerant to a wide range of water temperatures and could be transported easily in buckets and barrels across the whole of the US.

They do not grow as big as their cousin the largemouth bass, and though fish approaching ten pounds are occasionally taken the record of 11lb 15oz has stood since 1955. Sort of.

It was 9th July and David L. Hayes was spending the day with his wife and six-year-old son on Dale Hollow Lake, a vast man-made reservoir straddling the border of Tennessee and Kentucky which, when full, covers over 30,000 acres. Hayes was a bass fisherman of growing reputation particularly on Dale

Hollow where the deep clear water proved a challenge to most anglers.

At around mid-morning, while trolling a plug between two large weed-beds, Hayes had a thumping bite. At first he thought he had snagged the bottom but then the fish surged off. The fight was fairly long, mainly due to the fact that around a hundred yards of line was between angler and fish, but the bass was safely netted and then taken back to the dock at Cedar Hill resort where it was weighed and the true gravity of the catch first appreciated.

David Hayes was the new smallmouth bass record holder and remained so for forty years, though it was not another capture that saw his fish removed from the record books.

In 1996 an affidavit surfaced that had been written by a dock-hand at Cedar Hill in 1955 and claiming that the fish had been tampered with. It claimed that the fish had in fact weighed 8lb 15oz and that 3lb of lead weights and lumps of metal had been stuffed into the fish's belly before weighing. The affidavit claimed that local fishing guide Raymond Barlow had carried out the act without Hayes' knowledge, presumably with the intent of cashing in on the inevitable interest that such a fish would stir.

Hayes' record was immediately struck from the record lists, but the saga did not end there.

At 27 inches in length and 21^2/$_3$ inches in girth the dimensions of Hayes' fish pointed to a weight far in excess of 8lb 15oz. Further to that, Barlow's brother Ira (Barlow had died before the affidavit was discovered) claimed that Raymond had not even been at Cedar Hill on the day of the capture. Ira passed a polygraph test with this assertion.

Ron Fox of the Tennessee Wildlife Resources Agency conducted a thorough investigation into the capture and having spoken to various witnesses and the family of the Dockhand who wrote the affidavit, determined that Hayes' bass was indeed genuine and that false claims were made about its legitimacy by a disgruntled employee with a track record for telling fishy tales.

Hayes fish was not reinstated as a record for a further nine years, though fortunately he was still alive in 2005 to see the amendments made. Sadly, though the record still stands today, the controversy surrounding it still leaves the capture somewhat tarnished.

Though an affidavit is a statement made under oath, it is amazing how quickly the authorities and public opinion responded to its content. It is a sad reflection on human nature that we are so quick to judge one another and so happy to see those who have achieved be undermined or their success devalued.

We are not particularly good at dishing out unsolicited praise though we scream cynicism until our throats go dry. Some psychologists believe we project on to others the negative aspects that we dislike about ourselves, and that makes a great deal of sense, though we are also governed by our need to be taken seriously and may throw stones in a glass house so that no one else breaks our windows first.

Most people are competitive, and envy is a trait that can quickly cloud judgement. Many of those who were so quick to point the figure of suspicion at David Hayes were doing so out of twisted jealousy. They knew that they would never catch a smallmouth even close to that size and resented the fact that not only had someone else done so, but they had been receiving plaudits ever since.

Such attitude is present throughout society of course. If an athlete or cyclist fails a drug test then we seem to revel in their fall from grace. We are so quick to denounce them that sometimes it seems as though we have almost willed their downfall.

Fishermen are renowned for their tales and much of the envy or doubt within angling is borne from the fact that some anglers have and always will embellish the truth.

The Bailiwick Bass Club competition was won in July 2012 with a clonking bass that weighed thirteen pounds, earning the captor, a local Guernsey man, £800 for his efforts. One of his competitors recognised the distinct markings on the fish, however, and where he had seen it previously. Despite initial doubt from others his scepticism was proven to be correct - the bass had been stolen from the local aquarium the night before the match.

While prize money is an obvious carrot for a cheat's deceit, the angler also has the lure of 'fame', though this often blurs with infamy.

Angling is peculiar in that individuals can be held in almost mythical proportions within the sport but be absolutely anonymous outside it. We tend to hold anyone who catches a big fish in high regard and should anyone be regularly photographed with big fish then their name becomes synonymous with ability and expertise.

It is always nice to see your face in an angling magazine and it is equally nice to be recognised for the achievement, but some anglers get just a little bit too obsessed with stroking their ego and risk losing the true worth of their angle.

The digital age has made life a lot easier for the photographic forger (there is even an online App for faking fish photos) though dodgy snaps have always existed. A cardboard cut-out of a pike once fooled many and in 1990 one of the leading pike anglers in Britain was rumbled for having claimed photographs of three different pike which were actually all the same specimen.

Pike often seem to be the subject of fakery, and doubts were raised the moment a fuzzy image of a claimed 57lb specimen surfaced in 2009. A fish ten pounds bigger than the British record was always going to raise an eyebrow, but the poor quality of the photograph actually gave it some gravitas. If you are going to fake a picture then surely you would make a better job of it? These chaps didn't though, they were applying a double bluff and it wasn't until someone noticed the similarity between the pike in the photo and one in a pike fishing book that the truth finally unravelled. The picture in the book had been digitally stretched in order to add over twenty pounds to the fish, and in choosing a pike to work their mischief upon, the fraudsters were tapping into the fascination that every angler has had since childhood. We love tales of monsters, and the more farfetched the better the story sounds.

Our curiosity for fish may well be borne from the fact that they exist in a habitat that we cannot, but it is accentuated by the biological abilities of fish themselves. Warm-blooded mammals and birds grow to a typical size. There are always extremes and the odd freak but if you were to line up a hundred dunnocks there would be barely a feather to separate them.

Fish being cold-blooded, are far more reactive to their own environment and sensitive to the slightest of changes within it.

I kept a cold-water aquarium for many years and began with a dozen or so fish of various species. Over the years there were casualties, often in twos or threes, which I never replaced, but each time their number dwindled so the surviving fish grew. The growth spurt for each fish would be short and swift as they seemed to react almost immediately to the increase in space and reduction in competition. Eventually I was left with a rudd and a tench who were of a similar size when they first had the tank to themselves. I fed them flakes of food which would initially float and the rudd then bossed the tank with his upturned mouth and aptitude for surface feeding, quickly growing to twice the size of the tench.

After another few years the tench slipped off to the great estate lake in the sky and the rudd enjoyed another growth spurt. I believed now that the rudd must have reached his optimum size, but when we moved and my sister took on the aquarium and fitted it with a brand new oxygen pump he gained another ounce or two.

Though 'Ruddy' is no longer with is, I found it fascinating that his growth bore no relation to that of a mammal or bird. Though humans may grow outwards and lose a bit of height with the wear of old age, our skeletons reach their largest form and then stop. But for a handful of cases of hyperplasia, in which the growth hormone stays at an extreme level throughout (an inevitably shortened) life, our skeletal frame does not and cannot 'regrow'.

It wasn't the growth spurts that I found most interesting about Ruddy, but the fact that for periods of years he did not grow at all and yet would still react to a change in habitat.

Such adaptability is apparent when we fish. Certain waters

will produce bigger fish than others and the differences may be subtle. Oxygen levels, temperature and water acidity can all have major effects upon a fish's growth and with such fine lines there is always the chance that something gargantuan could be lurking almost anywhere.

Longevity is also a factor. In good water and with few stresses a carp can live for as long as a person, eels even longer. If within that time they maintain steady growth then they might reach colossal weights. The deep cold lochs in Scotland harbour enormous possibilities, as proven with the 39lb 8oz ferox trout foul-hooked and landed from Loch Awe in 1866.

If trout can grow that large, what about the pike? In the 1930s a skull found by the mouth of the river Endrick on Loch Lomond measured over a foot long suggesting it belonged to fish that weighed as much as seventy pounds. Enormous eels have been observed in Loch Ness including specimens at least six feet in length that were photographed by people looking for something a little bigger. They may actually have stumbled upon the truth behind the myth of the Loch Ness Monster, as local rumour tells of an eel ten feet in length found trapped in Foyers Power Station.

Such extremes give plausibility to possibility and never quash the beliefs we had as children of just what creatures might lurk in any form of water. Dry land monsters, the dragons and trolls, are filtered by reason long before we reach adulthood, yet the fish of our dreams remain tantalisingly possible.

Catching those fish is a serious business though, and one that some take to extremes. Anglers have always sought the biggest fish as Izaak Walton demonstrated with his method for chub fishing, but as more anglers clamour for the adulation of their peers so more suspicious captures seem to be made. It doesn't really matter how big a fish is, size really isn't everything. The 3lb 8oz perch that I caught on my first cast was trumped as 'fish of the day' by a pound and a halfer that Chris caught later in the afternoon. His fish looked astonishing. Most perch have five stripes, but this one wore seven and a bit. And the colours in each scale shimmered. My fish may have been larger but it was a bit tatty and washed out and we didn't spend nearly so long admiring it.

I do still care though about the size of a fish. I can't help but to. I don't weigh every fish I catch - far from it, but if a fish looks close to a landmark figure I will dig out my scales and then I am meticulous. Zero the scales; weigh the fish; weigh whatever was holding the fish; subtract the difference; then repeat the process if the margins are particularly fine and the fish is not suffering.

A common oversight particularly among inexperienced anglers is to forget to take off the weight of the net or sling in which they weighed their prize. I was once fishing a small weirpool and picking up a few fish when another angler spied my fortune and plonked himself down on the bank opposite. The pool itself is of a size that fits somewhere between being spacious enough for one or two anglers. As it was, I had been alternating between the sill and slack beneath my feet and the run-off into which the other angler now cast, but he wouldn't have known that and I was content to let him have the tail of the pool.

After an hour he had a bite and hooked a fish which came in with little trouble. It looked like a modest sized chub which he weighed in his monster 40-odd-inch landing-net with the handle still attached.

Another hour passed and I took a chunky barbel from under my feet which prompted a visit from the other angler. We exchanged pleasantries and I mentioned the fact he had caught a reasonable fish. "Six pounds," he said rather abruptly.

It is difficult to know what to say in such circumstances. I had presumed that he was inexperienced and he had confirmed the fact by mentioning that today was his first experience on running water, so it seemed plain that he had (unwittingly) included the weight of his net and handle in the weight of his chub. I didn't want a confrontation or to upset him, so made a vague comment about his fish having pulled the scales to nine pounds with the weight of the net to which he just frowned slightly and wandered off.

Such situations are tricky. A genuine mistake has been made and education is the best remedy for it, but how much responsibility did I want to take? He might not have responded well to someone pointing out a mistake and I didn't want my day sullied by any sort of abrasive exchange. Moreover why should I care? It had no effect on my life whatsoever, and yet it had clearly bothered me or I wouldn't be relating the tale now.

I suppose I was irked by the fact that I had never caught a six pound chub and knew how few and far between such fish were. At the time I reckoned to have caught at least seventy chub over five pounds and was miffed that this chap would go home having 'achieved' such a target on his first trip to a river.

Ultimately of course the incident would only affect me for as long as I let it. I would never see that angler again and never hear of his chub again, it was only ever going to be a problem to me if I let it be.

I once caught a barbel from the same stretch of water that

weighed 11lb 7oz. A good sized fish and yet one I nearly didn't bother weighing.

The bite had been a slight tightening of the line and I thought I had hooked a branch or lump of weed. Then the fish nodded a couple of times and I envisaged a bream, before an enormous, barbelled head came over the lip of the net.

It was a fish completely deformed. The front half was huge but it seemed to have been restricted around its middle for from the dorsal to the tail it looked like a 3-pounder.

The tail itself was tiny and the fish didn't seem to have much movement of it. I was fishing with Peter Arlott at the time, who had bailiffed the stretch for decades and never seen a fish quite like this one. He suggested I weigh it out of curiosity but when we put it back it looked as though it had swum its last.

It seemed to only be able to propel itself with its pectoral fins and a half-twitch of the back half of its body and was content to sit in the shallow water in the edge of the pool. Quite how it had lived this long was a mystery and Pete kept an eye on it through the night with half a mind that he might have to hoik it out and donk it on the head.

By morning it had swum off, and remarkably Pete caught it again two nights later when it once again came straight to the net like a sack of potatoes and then seemed happy to wallow around in the shallows. What amazed Pete the most was that he hadn't seen or heard of that fish before. The pool we were fishing was a tiny little mill pool with a run-off back to the main river that was only a couple of feet wide and inches deep. This banana-barbel had obviously found his way in there and stumbled upon the only place where he could survive with his deformities. The lack of flow, lack of predators and lack of competition meant that he could lollop about and live to a grand old age.

The capture left me a little uncertain. An eleven pound barbel was (and still is) a fish to be proud of and yet the condition of that poor old fish meant I felt unable to truly appreciate it. In time the relevance of that capture has increased mainly due to an increase of awareness of quite how many odds that fish had defied to live to such a size. He was not caught again, and Peter would surely have heard if he had been, and though time has most likely caught up with him now the fact that we made his acquaintance is a reminder of how tough life can be and how many elements create a successful capture.

Had I been a match angler then I would have had a different perspective altogether. I remember reading a match report in the 1980s about an angler who had caught an enormous roach during a match on the river Severn. When quizzed about the fish after the match he was dismissive and said he would have rather caught a 3lb 2oz chub than a 3lb 1oz roach because it would have given him a better chance of winning the match.

I couldn't quite believe the comment at the time but respected his candour and became intrigued by his mindset.

I began to follow match results more closely and my friend Leigh and I eventually decided to have a go. I don't think we held any genuine aspirations of winning, but rather naively thought that we could do okay.

The venue was the Basingstoke Canal and my dad dropped us off in time for the draw. We were pegged in opposite directions and by the looks of the map I had a long walk. Fortunately, someone else took pity on a thirteen-year-old lugging all his gear along the road and gave me a lift - which was just as well as it would have been a two-mile trek.

My fellow competitors were full of encouragement, praising the look of my peg and offering real hope that I should catch well. I was way out of my depth though, and a stiff crosswind meant that I couldn't cast to the far bank bush where I had balled in my groundbait. I decided to try with a ledger rod and swing-tip, but on taking it out of the bag I found the mid-section snapped in two - presumably while my gear was being squashed into the car earlier that morning.

Every other angler was using a pole and fishing delicate rigs on the far bank shelf. I decided my only option was to keep casting and hope to land the float in the right spot.

Eventually I did, the float sank and I bent into a solid fish. A lumpy bream rolled on the surface and I had sudden visions of glory, but the hook pinged and catapulted straight into the branches above me losing me my float too. I only had one float left in my box and didn't want to lose that as well so sat out the remainder of the match fishing the near bank where I caught a half-ounce perch just before the final whistle.

I weighed my monster in and started the long slog back to the car park to meet Leigh. He too had caught a solitary perch and though his was around the half-pound mark, he didn't weigh it in so technically I beat him.

We gave up on match fishing after that day satisfied that luck alone was never going to be enough to win any money. Successful match anglers need a serious amount of skill to turn in the consistent performances that they do. Alan Scotthorne and Bob Nudd have won nine world titles between them and that doesn't happen through good fortune alone. The commitment they possess in order to achieve such success is way beyond my capacity and I am quite grateful for it. Anglers are often pigeonholed, and well beyond fly, coarse and sea.

Coarse anglers are normally categorised as match, specimen or pleasure with plenty of sub-divisions thereafter, but the majority of fishermen don't really sit under any single umbrella. I fish for pleasure, but for the majority of the time I will target bigger individuals of whatever species I am fishing for. I have chased roach, barbel, chub, crucians and perch and while I have been happy to catch whatever comes along, I do like to know that there is the chance for something special.

What is vital is to apply context to wherever you are fishing, as that something 'special' can vary from river to river.

A four-pound chub would warrant little attention on the Lea or lower Dorset Stour but on a Yorkshire stream it is a big fish. Similarly a ten-pound barbel from the Kennet will raise few eyebrows whereas a similar weight from the Wye is a significant fish.

One of my favourite chapters in *Rod and Line* is entitled 'Fishing in Lilliput' where Arthur Ransome champions small stream fishing.

Ransome suggests that rivers such as the Test and Itchen give a distorted view of fishing and that not everyone is fortunate enough to fish such waters where a trout of a pound is a small fish. Instead, he champions the fishing to be found on those quiet hidden streams where there is no great pressure to catch and no huge fish to target. Sometimes, indeed, when the big rivers are out of order, many a man with a right to fish a nobler water had found himself well advised to leave that water and go to fish in Lilliput instead.

As Ransome goes on to explain, in Lilliput everything is small except you, which is fine as long as you adjust your mind and methods to suit. And while small fish will generally take a bait with far more gusto than their larger, wiser counterparts, by adjusting your own approach they can prove just as worthy an adversary.

Ransome would chase the trout of Lilliput with a single dry fly and would become as immersed in the challenge of rising a three-ounce fish as he would if it were three pounds.

My first Lilliputian casts were made in the mountain streams of Scotland. Some of these burns were little more than thin ribbon cascades that would fall vertically as much as they flowed horizontally. Yet wherever the water had bored out sufficient depth in the bedrock and the flow was not too punishing, small brown trout seemed to lie.

I didn't fish for them with a dry fly - in fact, I didn't use a fly at all - but instead would freeline worms and let the current find the fish. One burn on the Isle of Mull was so productive that I took home half a dozen and we ate them for breakfast. They were a fair size, between four and six ounces, and tasted sweet and clean; the flesh almost brilliant white. That was the only time I kept any Lilliputian trout for the pot as most burns were so small that removing any fish might have had a serious impact upon the ecosystem.

I did though once dispatch a deeply hooked trout to use as bait.

We were holidaying as a family on Eigg, the second largest of the Small Isles in the Inner Hebrides. Eigg only covers twelve square miles and is dominated by An Sgurr, a dramatic pitchstone shard that is sheer on three sides. The island is now owned by a trust which includes the islanders themselves and much has been done since the trust's formation in 1997 to improve facilities on the island.

Our holiday in the late 1980s was made in the days before mains electricity and the farmhouse we stayed in received limited power from a small hydro-generator in the burn which ran behind it.

The burn was tiny, narrow enough to step across and no more than a mile long as it bubbled down from the plateau behind the farm and swept in a wide bend before entering the sea. As well as providing power it also contained a good stock of little brownies and my brother Richard and I spent hours working our baits along the more gentle lower reaches. We had great fun, the only problem finding enough cowpats to turn over in order to grab the red-worms that the fish seemed to love.

Then, as we approached the end of our stay, Richard caught not only the biggest trout yet, he also spied an eel. The eel brought a brand new complexion to the stream. I had grown a little tired of catching the same trout from the same lies, and trips further afield to a lochen on the high moor and casts in the sea had proved fruitless. I was happiest fishing the little burn and my spirits were raised now that I had something different to target.

Worms were going to be no good as bait, the trout were too voracious but that deeply hooked fish was cut up into chunks too big for the brownies to swallow. Richard had seen the eel on the long straight where the stream was deepest (maybe fifteen inches) and steadiest. I found a spot where the bank overhung slightly and lowered my bait beneath it.

It was an hour before anything happened and then the rod tip flickered a couple of times before gently tweaking round. I simply lifted the rod and up came an eel. It was not even half a pound yet remains one of my proudest captures. A true monster of Lilliput.

Chapter Ten

Invisibility

The earth has music for those who listen.
GEORGE SANTAYANA

A survey by *Birdwatching* magazine in 2012 revealed a surprise number one in the search for Britain's favourite bird.

The robin, loveable bully of the bird-table and firm favourite for the title, found itself sitting in the number two spot, beaten by the bolt of blue himself, the kingfisher. I'm sure that the robin would not be too disappointed with his showing, after all there can be no shame finishing runner-up to a bird as stunning as the kingfisher.

The orange front would brighten any other bird and yet the iridescence that flashes from the blues of its back and wing tops seems so improbable in the sunlight that surely it is a handicap for the predatory hunter. Perhaps the fish are mesmerised by the colours, or mistake the blood red feet for coils of worms in the branches above them, or maybe the kingfisher is just so good at catching fish that he can afford the razzmatazz.

Another reason for the kingfisher's popularity is his supposed elusiveness. They are far from common admittedly, with a breeding population of some 6000 pairs, but they are also a bird that anglers get blasé about seeing.

I enjoy birdwatching and tend to take a pair of binoculars wherever I go. I am not a chaser of birds but more an opportunist, and spending time on the riverbank will always present opportunity. Binoculars, like fishing rods, are superb ice-breakers and if out walking, fellow birders will often smile and chat and share sightings. A kingfisher will frequently warrant mention alongside birds that I rarely if ever see, and yet because I so frequently share their environment I am never surprised to see one.

The call is familiar, the piped whistle that will pierce the chatter of other birdsong even from a fair distance. I have yet to have a kingfisher land on my rod, though they have often considered it and I once spent thirty seconds or so almost nose to beak with a bird that was trying to work out if I was really made of wood. I wasn't of course, I was watching chub from the branches of an alder and the kingfisher only fled when I could no longer suppress a smile. The chub sank away at the same moment, not because I was baring my teeth but because of the subtle change in atmosphere. Moments before I had been a benign presence, just another note making up the rhythm of the river, but as soon as I connected with the kingfisher I upset the beat. It may have been a momentary crackle that prompted me to smile, the kingfisher to flee and the chub to sink down into the roots but it was tangible nevertheless. In time I would breathe more gently, my pulse would settle and the chub would drift back from under my feet, then I would become invisible once more.

The village of Selborne sits on the edge of the South Downs National Park in east Hampshire where its 650 residents enjoy two pubs, a twelfth century church, a village shop and post office, and a steady stream of visitors whose main interest is a house called 'The Wakes'.

Previously a vicarage, 'The Wakes' now houses a museum honouring former resident Gilbert White, a parson whose interest in local natural history led to him being widely regarded as the first true ecologist. His studies in the eighteenth century, and more importantly the documentation of his studies (often in letters sent to fellow naturalists) led to major understandings of species behaviour. White recognised the importance of the earthworm in relation to soil quality and plant growth and he did much to dispel the common belief that swallows and martins didn't migrate but instead spent the winter buried in mud at the bottom of ponds and lakes. He did still ascertain that swallows might hibernate but that is quite a leap forward from the theory of their sub-aqua existence.

White also felt it important to focus upon study made in the field and not just of dead specimens in a laboratory. He differentiated similar bird species such as willow warbler and chiffchaff by their song and behaviour and wrote excitedly of the arrival of the wonderfully named pettichaps (lesser whitethroat to you and I) in his garden.

What is sadly apparent from his observations is the impact Man has subsequently had upon so many species that were once widespread. White writes of bustards on the South Downs and locally nesting moor buzzards (marsh harriers) but his methods of field study were unusual and the most common method of identification was to shoot first and look later:

Selborne, May 7, 1779
It is now more than forty years that I have paid some

attention to the ornithology of this district, without being able to exhaust the subject: new occurrences still arise as long as any inquiries are kept active.

In the last week of last month five of those most rare birds, too uncommon to have obtained an English name, but known to naturalists by the terms of himantopus, *or* loripes, *and* charadrius himantopus, *were shot upon the verge of Frinsham-pond, a large lake belonging to the bishop of Winchester, and lying between Woolmer-forest, and the town of Farnham, in the county of Surrey. The pond keeper says there were three brace in the flock; but that, after he had satisfied his curiosity, he suffered the sixth to remain unmolested.*

The black-winged stilt (*Himantopus himantopus*) to which White is referring is a long-legged wading bird found in central-south-eastern Europe, central Asia and Africa. It occurs as a vagrant in this country with typically five or fewer records per year.

From the extract above, it is clear that the bird had a similar status in White's day, and yet the pond-keeper at Frensham had no qualms about shooting five of the six birds he found to 'satisfy his curiosity'.

Though the outcome was unfortunate, what this tale does suggest is that with such black and white thinking many birds and animals would have behaved in Gilbert White's time much as the fish responded to Francis Francis' horsehair line. They wouldn't get a second chance so were less likely to spot danger and White would have been able to observe and study far closer than naturalists today. The population of Britain would have been around 7 million in White's day, and with no intensive farming or industrial pollution the natural environment would have been incredibly healthy.

Today, with a ten-fold increase in population and an ever more clinical approach to agriculture and development, we have squeezed the life out of much of our countryside. Huge fields may produce more yield but they act like deserts for wildlife, particularly with fungicides and pesticides proving so efficient.

For many years the decline in some of our more iconic species has gone unnoticed. Kestrels seemed to hover over every motorway verge and yet this wasn't an indication of their profligacy, we had simply pushed them out of their natural lowland habitats. The thin strips of rough grass and scrub beside our trunk roads were the last corridors of sanctuary for many of the insects and small mammals that make up the kestrel's prey.

As a result, never before have our waterways been so important for our wildlife. Though we have tried our very best to manipulate and dictate the flow of all our streams and rivers, the simple fact is that water can never be fully harnessed. Current figures suggest that one in six of the homes in Britain are at risk from flooding and this is largely due to the fact that we have tackled over-population by claiming cheap land that we should have left to nature. This is of no consolation to the millions of people whose lives have been torn apart by the extensive floods of the early twenty-first century, but it is a reminder that Mother Nature is more resilient than we give her credit for.

Water is relentless. Springs have reappeared after lying dry for decades and as the rivers have risen so they have sought the old ditches and flood-plains that man has tidied away. For all of the destruction and heartbreak that water can cause it remains a life-blood for so much ecology. Plants grow unhindered, invertebrates unsprayed and with the base of the food chain intact so every step above can thrive.

River valleys offer a glimpse into the world that Gilbert White would have walked and anglers the chance to see a world through his eyes. We are privileged, though sometimes we may not appreciate the fact.

At the end of the nineteenth century a close season was introduced for coarse angling. With the majority of fish being caught and killed, it was determined that fishing be outlawed through the spring when the fish were most likely to spawn.

The close season has always been contentious within angling circles as many believe it to be futile and archaic while the conservation minded believe its existence to have deeper environmental importance than the protection of fish.

Through the second half of the twentieth century came growth in the creation and management of coarse fisheries. Demand for gravel increased with the expansion of the road network and some river valleys became dotted with pits that formed ideal habitats for aquatic life. Stillwater angling was growing in popularity but as more landowners cashed in so calls for a change in the close season law grew ever louder.

A forced closure of three months (mid March to mid June) had an enormous impact on revenue, especially as that period came after winter when many anglers hang up their rods. Some parts of Britain, Devon and Cornwall for example, had never operated a close season and here landowners and farmers cashed in by digging lakes and filling them with fish. Elsewhere, fishery owners overcame the restriction by introducing 'any-method trout-fishing', stocking their waters with trout, which were in season, and letting people catch them on coarse gear. This was perfectly legal, but made the close season something of a farce. As long as trout were present in a lake then people could fish for them in any way they saw fit and would 'accidently' catch the coarse fish that they were truly targeting.

In 1995 close-season restrictions were lifted on stillwaters and in 2000 this was extended to canals, sensible actions in light of angling direction and interest. Commercial fisheries could operate with a twelve-month income (some choosing to close in mid-winter for maintenance work when few anglers would want to fish) and, as importantly, tackle shops could survive more easily in a world of shrinking economies and cheap mail-order delivery.

The tackle shop plays a vital role in angling but has suffered greatly from the rise of the internet. Before moving west, my favourite tackle shop was in Tadley, some thirty miles from home but close to the Kennet where I spent so many hours. I would walk in and be greeted like an old friend, the kettle was always boiling and my business appreciated whether I bought a packet of hooks or a gallon of maggots. Aside from the pleasure of the welcome, the shop was also a mine of information. River conditions, water temperature, recent catches; anything that had happened of interest in the valley would be discussed in the shop and the owner (another Kevin) would be just about the most knowledgeable man in the county.

Internet forums may provide an offshoot from the traditional tackle-shop grapevine but you are still likely to hear whispers that would never be discussed openly.

There are sufficient anglers fishing stillwaters through the spring for these shops to maintain turnover. Fortunate, because it is vital that the close season remains on our rivers.

A river provides a rich but delicate environment and the manner in which we tend to fish can have a varying effect upon it. A fly fisherman in spring will be mobile and relatively unobtrusive. He will cover a lot of water, sometimes from within it, but is unlikely to fish on wet days when there is little in the way of fly-life to imitate.

The coarse angler on the other hand is more sedentary and less bothered about getting rained on and while his presence on the opening day of the season causes little interruption to the flow of life, it is because for three months he hasn't been treading the banks.

After a wet winter with the river often over its banks, some swims resemble the Somme rather than a riverbank. Big boots have squelched the ground into a muddy mess and were they to continue to tread through the spring then the bankside plants would not regenerate and pull everything back together within their root structures. Without the plants the bank itself would crumble into the water, colouring the water and blocking the sunlight which is so important to the growth of the cress and crowfoot which support the river's ecology. Fewer plants means fewer invertebrates and fewer fish as a result, and while this would be localised, these specific spots would be where the river is at its richest, hence the fact that anglers frequent them. Changing the dimension of such a small part of an ecosystem can have a massive effect on the whole and it is in the anglers' interest to maintain the structure and order, particularly when so many rivers suffer so much from over-extraction and mis-management.

When we return to the rivers in June the sand martins and kingfishers and moorhens have already made their nests and most are feeding young that they will not abandon. Were people present in April and May when they were looking to create a clutch then the birds would not have stayed, and while the level of impact would be hard to quantify, the fact that there would be any impact at all is reason enough to avoid the situation.

The fish themselves do not refer to a calendar to breed and instead respond to the subtle changes in their watery home. After a cold spring, chub and barbel will still be spawning well into the summer, but they do at least have an environment intact and sufficiently established in which to make successful spawning.

Every river is different of course, and the presence of anglers would have far less impact on a tidal stretch of the river Trent than on an intimate reach of the Sussex Rother, but ultimately the need for a close season has gone far beyond the welfare of the fish. So much occurs on a riverbank in spring that the angler benefits from the break as well as the environment. The contrast between a March quagmire and a June masterpiece is absolute and because the world is so different when we return in early summer, we make our intrusion as gentle as we are able.

Thick bankside growth is to an angler's advantage. He can nudge a rod-tip between the meadowsweet and willowherb and lower a bait beneath our feet without raising so much as a fin-flick of concern from the fish below. Then let himself sink into the image, become part of it and not an interloper seeking to displace the balance.

The beauty in such a situation is that as the dry world continues to move around you, so the wet world in which we have our interest also turns, without being disturbed.

A fish survives through instinct and will react in kind to any panic it feels above the water's surface. If a water-vole is contentedly paddling along the edge of a reed-bed then all is well. If ducks or swans are drifting with wings tucked in and webbed feet gently steering then there is no threat to fear.

As an angler becomes ever more ensconced into this world then so his own senses heighten. We can creep and crawl and whisper our way into position but our purpose will still give our game away. By this point of the day our aims and need to catch a fish have been diluted by the rhythm of the water, but while we might appear less driven we are actually ever more potent.

No matter what our intention or inclination, we can never hide the fact that we are natural predators. Our fixed, forward-facing eyes will always give us away. We care little for what is behind us, only the prey before us, and regardless of our thoughts, laying both eyes upon a creature implies total attention and reason enough for that creature to fear.

Body language is a clear indication of motive. If we stand square to another person then we are encouraging physical interaction, be it aggression or affectionate, so our normal approach to others is more open - sideways on and threat free.

Our approach to horses demonstrates the point. Horses are by nature affectionate and inquisitive and will wander up to strangers with these traits in mind. Our general response is to face up to them and try and plonk a hand on their nose, not the most amiable of greetings. Instead, if we turn side-on and allow the horse to sniff us (which is why it comes nose first, not because it has itchy nostrils) then they will feel more comfortable and trusting.

This approach is welcomed across the natural world and in time becomes routine. Walks around my local hills will take me through fields of sheep, animals that do not need much encouragement to take flight. It is a nice feeling therefore, to be able to pass through a flock without causing any disturbance other than a couple of cursory glances. On one occasion this winter I walked a nearby hill in filthy weather and one of the ewes actually approached me. I let it come and left a loose hand by my side which it did not just sniff but also nuzzled before wandering back to the flock. A sheep may not be a wild animal but if you carry no threat then any creature's natural curiosity is likely to override their fear or aggression.

A kestrel once landed on a post around fifty yards ahead on the path I was walking and though it moved to fly a couple of times as I approached, instead it opted to wait and see what I was about. I managed to walk right up to the bird, until our faces were just four or five feet apart and the kestrel was as curious of me as I of it.

She was a female and was fascinated by my face, not least my eyes which she kept peering forward to get a better look at. We studied one another for perhaps thirty seconds before I spooked her by, for some unknown reason, raising a fist to her as would a falconer.

It was a peculiar move on my part, not least because I was bare-handed. A tawny owl once nearly crushed my finger so I was well aware of the damage that talons can inflict, but I obviously decided she would have understood my gesture and she settled on my fist without so much as a scratch.

Raptors are familiar to many anglers and spending so much time in such good hunting habitat makes us more likely to stumble on the less familiar.

This past winter I watched two ravens mobbing a goshawk, and in previous years I have seen marsh harrier, peregrine and hobbies alongside the more familiar species. Barn owls are lovers of water meadows, particularly in winter, and there are some locations where you can expect to see them.

Of course, it isn't just birds of prey. I once almost trod on a bittern who obviously liked the look of a favourite perch hole, and the pained cries of the water rail is a sound synonymous with reed-beds. I may still be waiting for a kingfisher to perch on my rod, but plenty of other species have made use of this temporary perch. Marsh tit and reed bunting have cocked a sideways glance at me as they realise they have landed on something not entirely natural, while Britain's former favourite the robin can sniff a pint of maggots out from miles away.

In parts of Europe, where small birds are heavily persecuted, the robin is very much a skulking bird. Keeping a low profile much like its close relative the dunnock. In Britain however, he has an altogether different attitude. He is brash, dominant and almost fearless of man, and few anglers begrudge sharing some bait with him, even if he is a little demanding. Even on remote stretches of unfished river a winter robin will approach an angler and sing for his dinner.

People are suckers for the cute, be they feathered or furry, and otters will always get folk gushing. Some anglers are less than impressed with the remarkable rise in the otter's fortunes though, and some fisheries and garden ponds have been cleaned out by these furred fishermen. Otters are present in every county of Britain, benefitting from reintroductions in the Eighties and Nineties and more importantly a status of protection. The impact they have had on local fish stocks undeniable but perhaps this is more of a reflection of the overall condition of our waterways. After all, a healthy river should be able to support predators *and* prey.

At least the otters tend to push mink numbers down. Mink are non-native mustelids that have found our habitat to their liking having escaped (and been 'freed' by animal rights activists) from farms where they were kept largely for their fur. They are voracious hunters that have caused havoc to our native wildlife. One summer on a swollen Kennet I watched a group of six work their way through an entire colony of sand martins. The water level was high enough for the mink to get into the martin's burrows and despite my presence (and a few stones lobbed in their direction) they made short work of eggs and chicks.

Mink have also had an enormous impact on our water-vole population, contributing towards a ninety-five per cent reduction in the vole population in sixty years. Yellow teeth aside, the water-vole is a delightful rodent with a neat doggy-paddle and a demeanour of gentle purpose that so inspired Ratty in Kenneth Grahame's *Wind in the Willows* - a rodent who loved nothing more than drifting down a stream on his boat.

Whether you get away, or whether you don't; whether you arrive at your destination or whether you reach somewhere else, or whether you never get anywhere at all, you're always busy, and you never do anything in particular; and when you've done it there's always something else to do, and you can do it if you like, but you'd much better not.

A day on a boat with a water-vole sounds rather like a day fishing and in those places where voles still survive, their carefree ways can be a delight to witness. I have spent many days in the company of water-voles and they never seem concerned at my presence. They are steady if slow swimmers and noisy gnawers, but always a treat when fishing.

A better swimmer than a vole is the grass snake, an animal less close to the nation's heart. Our largest reptile, the grassie is a lover of water, feeding almost exclusively on amphibians. Britain is at the northern edge of their range, with none in Ireland (after St Patrick shooed them out) and just a handful nudging into southern Scotland. They are a cracking prize for an angler and will come remarkably close if undisturbed.

My favourite of many encounters came on a canalised stretch of the Kennet, when Martin let me share his secret swim.

The stretch of river is hugely underfished, with most anglers far more interested in the pacier, barbel-rich waters up- and downstream. Martin had fished it a few times in the company of Derek, who a few years previously had sadly succumbed to cancer. Derek's favourite swim was beneath a near-bank ash where he laid on with a float and caught big roach, perch, chub and barbel, but though Martin had mentioned it many times it was some years before we ventured to fish it by ourselves.

The swim, when we found it, was all but unfishable though, the undergrowth having tangled into the water since Derek's final cast. We could have tidied it, cut back the branches and wet a line, yet it seemed quite fitting to leave it to the river and instead we headed downstream. I plonked myself into the first likely spot and paid for my laziness catching just a solitary perch all afternoon. Martin fared better a couple of hundred yards further on where he caught perch, chub and a clonking carp of nearly twenty pounds and we decided to return the following day and both fish Martin's swim.

The swim was wonderfully intimate. For two or three hundred yards the undergrowth was thick enough to all but conceal any evidence of the river, and a few bent stalks left by Martin the day before were the only sign of human activity. His faint path led us to a small gap between willow and an ash where a thin line of reeds looked over a strip of lily-pads around six feet across. There was a shelf under the furthest pads where the water deepened to around four and a half feet and here we lowered in a few bait-dropper fulls of hemp and casters before laying on with overshotted floats and casters on the hook.

The action was far from frenetic but bites came steadily. The first fish to show were perch before a couple of decent roach added variety. All then went quiet so we topped up the loose-feed and within minutes the lily-pads began twitching as better fish poked around the stems below. I hooked a long, lean chub of nearly five pounds and moments later Martin had a tench of a similar size that bored hard into the weed beneath our feet. Another chub and tench followed before the swim went quiet again and we decided to rest it and put the kettle on.

We had caught some lovely fish and as we sipped our tea we reflected on the fact that they were likely never to have been caught before. With mugs drained we returned to the fishing and it was then that the grass snake appeared. It wasn't a particularly big grassie, not quite thirty inches, and he worked upstream across the lilies completely unaware of us. A flick of his tongue caught our scent though and he clocked us, immediately pushing off the pads and into the main river. The flow took him by surprise and he was whisked a yard downstream before he stablilised and tried to work upstream against the current.

After a couple of seconds of hard swimming he turned to come into the bank only to see us still there. The flow was countering his progress perfectly and no matter how hard he tried he simply couldn't swim away from us. A snake's eye normally seems cold and piercing, but this grass-snake was showing a wealth of expression. He kept looking at us, frowning because we were still there and then dropping his head to get as much body beneath the surface and get away. The pattern continued for at least a minute and Martin and I were trying our best not to fall over laughing.

Eventually the snake gave up plan B and reverted to plan A, slipping across the pads and coming on to land almost between my feet with a look somewhere between disdain and utter confusion . . .

Chapter Eleven

The Witching Hour

The pale stars were sliding into their places. The whispering of the leaves was almost hushed. All about them it was still and shadowy and sweet. It was that wonderful moment when, for lack of a visible horizon, the not yet darkened world seems infinitely greater - a moment when anything can happen, anything be believed in.

OLIVIA HOWARD DUNBAR, THE SHELL OF SENSE

Of our senses it is sight that we invariably trust the most and in turn the one we most fear losing, yet it is also the most easily deceived. We may taste, smell, hear or feel something that is unpleasant but our cognitive self will make a mental note of the look of that thing so that our eyes warn us first should we encounter it again. As a result our other senses will have a pre-conceived notion of a situation based upon what our sight has already determined. Ice cream is cold, a mug of tea hot and a balloon will go BANG! when it bursts.

The remaining senses of those people without the use of sight are said to develop more keenly as a result. This stands to reason, but is it a result of the brain channelling more resources through those remaining nerve endings or evidence of the minds of the sighted becoming lazy from a reliance on their dominant sense?

When we cannot physically see something in its totality, then we will let our imagination fill in the gaps, either with images from the past or presumption. If a plate of food looks like a

173

dog's dinner then it is difficult to taste it without Pedigree Chum in mind.

Man's dependence upon sight means he is also dependent upon light. The optic nerves carry messages to the brain decoded from the light received by photoreceptor cells in the eye. As light levels drop, our eyes 'play tricks on us', though in reality it is the brain misinterpreting the information that it is receiving. Without a working harmony between the brain and the eye our minds are liable to err towards panic and fear - darkness becomes something to dread so we put the lights on.

Any angler knows that spending a day outside and letting your eyes adjust naturally to failing natural light will allow your night vision to function far more efficiently. Our photoreceptors are made up of rods and cones the latter of which determine colour while the former receive images in black and white. Many animals have more rods than us meaning less colour determination but superior vision in low light conditions, though without the interruption of artificial light the rods in our eyes can allow us sharper night-time definition than we may realise.

This is just as well, because for an angler a setting sun is not a signal to head for home but is in fact the prelude to the most productive period of the day.

Low light is the very best light to fish in. Bright sunshine can make the sub-surface world too perilous for fish to do anything other than tuck up in a weed-bed or sunken castle. As the sun dips these fish will look to feed in comparative safety, and seemingly empty swims can come alive. Predator fish, such as the perch, will also stir as their prey begin to move, using the shadows from which to launch an ambush.

The atmosphere begins to crackle as diurnal life makes way for the mysteries of night. So much is happening and yet the intensity is centred upon your float, as you strain your eyes slightly and the fading red of the tip begins to dance. It is the angler's witching hour, but the witches will have to wait.

The 'witching hour' is most popularly regarded as that time around midnight when ghouls and warlocks work their mischief. The notion is centuries old; Shakespeare made reference to it in *Hamlet* - 'Tis now the very witching time of night' - while Mary Shelley mentioned it in her introduction to the 1831 edition of *Frankenstein* - 'Night waned upon this talk, and even the witching hour had gone by, before we retired to rest.'

More well known is Washington Irving's use of the term in his 1835 tale *The Legend of Sleepy Hollow*:

> *Then, as he wended his way by swamp and stream and awful woodland to the farmhouse where he happened to be quartered, every sound of Nature at that witching hour fluttered his excited imagination . . .*

Irving's references to the witching hour seem to suggest no specific time, but instead that period when the imagination is most easily led. When the most subtle of sounds conjure up images of the unearthly, and shadows shield the sinister.

So many tales of ghosts are spun in the half-light, when the silent flight of a barn owl can look otherworldly and tree stumps seem to move as they lose definition. Through history twilight has been prime time for the creation of legends and it is interesting that both Mary Shelley and Washington Irving are likely to have been influenced by German folk tales.

Shelley refers to a collection of German ghost stories that she and her companions would tell to one another during the summer evenings of 1816 which she spent in Geneva. Irving, on the other hand, spent seventeen years in Europe where it is likely that he was affected by tales of the Wild Hunt.

Legends that cross the barriers of language and culture are difficult to source, though their widespread recounts give them deeper substance. Tales of great swathes of ghostly spectres who hunt across darkening skies are told across northern and central Europe. These Wild Hunts are led by different figures dependent upon where you are - the Norse believed they were led by Odin whereas in Britain, King Arthur, St Guthlac and even Sir Francis Drake are among those said to lead the company of the dead. The purpose is invariably sinister; either seeking out souls or heralding imminent doom, and many legends suggested that anyone unfortunate enough to witness the Wild Hunt would die thereafter; one of those rather handy disclaimers that ensure no witness to an event can ever be found.

In the modern day we still attach belief to such myths - the idea that drowning is 'pleasant' or that if you die in a dream then you die in real life are popularly told and widely believed despite the fact that there would be a distinct lack of witnesses to attest to them.

What is more easy to believe is that a stormy twilight can twist the imagination into the most peculiar of forms. The sudden change in air pressure can thump around our heads and electricity in the atmosphere can make our hairs stand on end and leave us wide eyed. If the clouds are dark and billowing and the air rushes almost as loudly as the thunder then people can be easily convinced of something extraordinary happening

- especially with the dog hiding under the table and the neighbour's horses charging around as if possessed. In the split second illumination of lightning our mind is expecting to see something terrifying and as a result will do just that.

The 'witching hour' is a phrase well coined, but it does serve to describe the movements of less fantastical creatures. We might not believe in phantoms and cockatrices but still we feel that spark by the water when the monsters below the surface begin to move.

Nightwalk was Chris Yates' first published step away from fishing. There were odd murmurs of dismay from those who had long treasured his words on water but there was no basis for panic. The subject matter may have changed a touch but the lyrical style was as strong as ever. Richer, if truth be told:

> *When I was a child, my parents would take my sister, brother and me for long Sunday walks through the fields and woods that began at the end of our street, but we were nearly always home before dark. In midwinter, however, when the sun sets at four in the afternoon, we would sometimes find that the dark had overtaken us. Though my parents tried to avoid such lateness, I liked the way the orderly landscape seemed to grow wilder and more mysterious as the twilight faded; and I liked how the prospect of darkness chased everyone else away long before us so that it appeared we were walking through an uninhabited country - uninhabited, except of course for the local fauna.*

It may seem an alien notion to some, but Chris' desire to embrace the darkness of night is an enlightening one. I feared the dark for many years and well into adulthood. I cannot recall a specific event that may have triggered it, but looking back I can't help but wonder if my mind that had been tormented by depression found a lightless void simply too much to bear. The sticky dread that would occasionally overwhelm me was definitely not driven by the possibility of werewolf or bear attacks and I reasoned that if it were a fear of a person stepping menacingly from the shadows then that would at least be more rational and possible; an anxiety not helped by a pretty unpleasant encounter with three thugs on a dark side-street in New Cross when I was eighteen. A random attack might not be personal, but it isn't any less traumatic.

As I overcame depression so too eased the insomnia that is both symptom and compound of the illness. Night-time is a cold, lonely place when your thoughts echo the darkness, but with sleep and sweeter dreams came a freshened perspective.

This benefitted my fishing no end. I could make a dash for the river after a working day and make plunder rather than haste when the sun set.

I was obsessing with barbel around that time, and evening, particularly last light, was the very best time to have a bait in the water. I had been finding success fishing over beds of stewed wheat and having boiled up a fresh, garlic-infused batch, took half a bucketful along to the river.

I headed for a favourite swim and piled in the bait knowing that at some point in the day the fish would arrive and that they wouldn't be able to resist the wheat when they did.

By mid-afternoon, after six biteless hours and the sun high in a cloudless sky, I was getting anxious, but decided to go for broke and topped up the swim with more bait. I didn't get a touch until the light began to fade, and then for an hour I experienced extraordinary fishing. I landed seven barbel, lost two to hook pulls and let Martin (who had been fishing further down-river) take a couple of fish while I was unhooking or playing one of my own. I couldn't get a bait in fast enough and waited no more than a minute for a bite during that golden time. The witches would not be waiting in the dark on the way back to the car after an hour like that.

I was, though, reliant on artificial light to pack up and find my way back across the fields and it wasn't until I spent time fishing with Chris Yates that I found the value in leaving the torches and lanterns at home. Chris, as he describes in *Nightwalk*, relies entirely upon his own night-vision when darkness descends, whereas the majority of people will reach for unnatural assistance the moment anything begins to smudge. If your eyes have adjusted gradually to diminishing light then it is quite possible (unless tying knots or sorting severe tangles) to fish into total darkness even when the moon is obscured. With the rods that make up our photoreceptors being allowed to filter images in their own two-tone time so they are more effective and efficient. Just a couple of seconds of pollution from a torch or mobile phone will raise the cones once more, though, as they rush to determine colours and definition. Suddenly the night will become twice as dark.

Last summer Chris and I were fishing for crucians and an angler on the opposite bank was flicking on a headtorch each time he checked his bait or made a cast. Though the light source was distant and relatively subtle, I found myself shielding my eyes like a vampire in a Hammer horror - I may even have hissed. Light draws our gaze when it is scarce, as any driver will know if an oncoming car has its lights on full-beam; you can't help but dazzle yourself.

Astigmatism will always limit my night vision to some degree but as long as I get myself vaguely organised before dark, I can fish through twilight without any need for a torch.

The key is to have things to hand and ensure that there are no stray packets of hooks or disgorgers lying easy to miss in the grass by your feet. It is also possible to position yourself in such a way so as to make out your float against the reflection of the western sky. Fingers of white will hold above the horizon long after the sun has set, and a dark tipped float will stand out well in the glassy mirror of the water's surface.

If you are facing east or intending to fish on into the night itself, then a glowstick or isotope attached to the top of the float is a fantastic way to fish. The glowstick is attached to the float with a short rubber tube and activated by bending it until the inner capsule snaps releasing the second of two contained chemicals. The ensuing reaction excites a dye which in turn releases a photon of light. The specific quantities of chemicals will determine how long and how brightly light will be produced, but it is limited and cannot be reused. Because the sticks glow rather than shine, the light produced is soft and does not transfer itself beyond a few inches, thus allowing a fisherman to watch it without losing his night vision.

If ledgering or freelining, and bite alarms or silver foil bobbins are not your thing, then feeling the line for bites is as exciting as fishing gets. In the gloom the line looped around your fingers begins to feel more and more alive. You become so aware of the possibility that rather like a dancing float you begin to imagine bites. Then, when the line actually tweaks for real, the effect is like a poke in the ribs.

When fishing for chub, touch-ledgering is one of the most effective methods of bite indication. Chub are wary fish and tend to pick baits up in their lips before deciding whether it is safe. Soft baits such as cheese-paste will sometimes show the indentations where the bait has been mouthed and rejected when the chub felt resistance. When feeling for bites it is actually possible to 'feed' a tentative chub a little slack line when that first delicate twitch is felt. It may go against your intuition to give slack line when a fish is apparently biting, but it can often fool the spookiest of chub.

Surface fishing can be frenetic after the sun sets as dry-fly anglers in particular will testify. Fly-hatches are often at their most intense in the evening as the insects emerge in vast clouds in the hope of using the half-light to avoid predation by birds and bats. Clouds of hirundines (swallows, martins) and swifts will gather over chalkstreams at dusk, feasting on the hatch before the bats take over in the pitch black. Trout can feed with abandon at such times and sport can be brisk after a slow sunny day.

Other fish will also respond to this sudden food source. I used to fish a small lake that sat alongside the chalkstream that fed it. It would have regular hatches through the summer but one early season evening, after a cold spring, I arrived to find clouds of mayfly billowing across the surface. The noise was intense and the carp were going bananas. It had been a breezy day and the pond surface was littered with seed-heads and clocks which fish were crashing into amid the frenzy of mayfly. I was too fascinated to actually fish, though I could have caught on a bare hook had I wanted.

On another balmy summer evening while fishing a different lake, the carp had followed a hatch into a reeded corner where I managed to switch their interest from insects to dog biscuits and floating crust. I was still catching well after dark and as the carp started to ease off so the tench moved in. These traditionally bottom feeding fish were far from adept at slurping down lumps of bread but made a good enough job so I managed to hook a fair few.

This feeding pattern will often repeat itself. Fish that are feeding confidently during the witching hour will continue to do so well into the night. Though many pressured fish, particularly carp, will use darkness almost exclusively in which to feed, physical blackness isn't always a trigger for fish to let their guard down.

Arthur Ransome was curious as to a fish's reaction to a solar eclipse, and having found nothing documented decided to find out for himself.

The total eclipse of June 29th, 1927 was the first to be witnessed on the British mainland for over two hundred years. Much was previously written of the effect of an eclipse on the behaviour of cattle and birds and Ransome decided he would us this unique opportunity to cast for trout. It required a bending of water rules to be on his chosen tarn at five-thirty in the morning but he figured that few would mind given the circumstances. The trout were showing and he managed to catch a small one shortly before the light began to change.

Everything went suddenly dark. The noise of curlews, pewits, and small upland birds stopped. There was absolute silence, and it was as if a roof had suddenly been put over the tarn.

The sheep on the mountain had stopped feeding while the

tarn was dead. No trout rose during the darkness of the eclipse and Ransome likened the effect to that of a fisherman casting his shadow over a shoal of wary fish.

It was twenty minutes after the shadow had passed back into daylight that trout again began to rise, and it is interesting that their reaction was so absolute. Fish feed well on the dullest of days, yet total darkness is seemingly a step too far. Predators such as the otter, which, until its recent spread at least, is primarily a nocturnal hunter, have too much of an edge in pitch darkness. Their super-sensitive whiskers can lead them to prey under stones and in the thickest of weed-beds, so fish that are sight dependent will do well to keep a low profile.

Though a fish might struggle to see an otter coming in the dark, were it on land then it could probably smell it. Later that same evening that Chris and I were dazzled by the headlight-wielding angler on the far bank, we got a full nose of *eau d'otter*. The torch flasher had gone and we had fished on into the late hours, eighty yards or so apart and both having had a couple of fish.

We were waiting for one another to call time, and when I heard footsteps approaching I thought Chris was coming down to suggest we leave. Either that or he had just caught a big crucian. A big, smelly crucian. My word, the stench that walloped me in the face was enough to turn my stomach. For a moment I was puzzled, but then a big dog otter trotted passed me taking his spectacular musk with him. Chris it turned out had experienced an identical encounter: hearing me coming down the bank only to find I had grown fur and rolled in rancid fish guts.

I was relieved to have seen the source of the stench; had it remained a mystery then my imagination might have started to wander. And though I am far less fearful of things that go bump in the night than I was twenty years ago, rationality can still be unsettled by circumstance. And when anxieties are shared . . .

A decade or so ago, Martin and I were spending a week targeting barbel on the Kennet. It was July and we were seriously well prepared. Martin never approaches anything half-heartedly and we had a sack of hempseed, a sack of particle blend, maggots, casters, pellets, peculiar paste baits and a lot of Spam.

We began the week on well trodden banks and found plenty of fish. Barbel and chub were coming regularly to the net, but after four days we hankered after something a little different. Despite a good amount of barbel, we were yet to encounter anything approaching gargantuan and the popular stretches, while holding plenty of fish, were just too popular.

Flicking through the club book we found one stretch that looked as though it might offer the chance of solitude and adventure. Martin had been a club member for many years and had never fished it nor met anyone who had. The main deterrent was the isolation. Parking was over a mile from the river which, according to rumour, was sluggish and overgrown and not worth the effort.

On the plus side this stretch did allow night fishing, and though we did not intend to angle our way until dawn, we had grown frustrated at having to pack up on other reaches just when the fish were starting to move.

The fifth morning of our week saw us pointing the car down an unmarked track and into the unknown. It was exciting, though we soon regretted the half ton of bait and all the gear we had brought; none of which we wanted to leave in the car where it might invite theft.

The walk was tough: no footpath but three or four fences to get over and then a riverbank that clearly hadn't been walked that season. The undergrowth was every bit as thick as the rumours had suggested but the river itself looked good. One swim in a small copse looked particularly inviting with a hole beneath a near-bank tree offering sanctuary and easy fishing. I baited it with a mixture from the bucket and left it to fester.

Martin fancied a swim further upstream where a fallen tree had created a cracking looking eddy in mid-river. The added advantage of his spot being just beyond the treeline was the lack of undergrowth, quite handy when the nettles were swaying at head height where I was fishing.

The day drifted quietly by, and in hot, bright conditions we had expected little action. As the sun dipped we started to focus more earnestly though, and just before dark I had a sharp jag on the rod-tip. Suspecting chub I recast and waited for another chance. After fifteen minutes the line tightened and I was into a fish which rolled on the surface and managed to snag the hook link over a trailing branch. I could see a fair size tail slapping against the surface in the moonlight, and thinking I had a serious chub on, prepared to strip off and get wet. I didn't have to worry, though, the fish kicked itself free and after a couple of mild lunges I bundled it into the net. It was a bream, leaving me disappointed but grateful that I hadn't taken a swim for him.

The next bite was certainly not a bream. It came an hour or so later just as I was losing heart, and a short sharp dink on the rod-tip was followed by an almighty heave. I was using 10lb line but this fish was going to take some stopping and the reel screamed as it tore off downstream under the stump and into the under-cut bank where everything went solid. I dropped the rod-tip under the surface, inched myself as close to the water as possible without getting wet and applied as much pressure as I dared.

The resistance was steady but just as I thought it had thrown the hook, so the fish kicked a couple of times to let me know I was still in contact. I have learnt to my cost in such situations that patience is vital, and steady but continual pressure on a fish is often the best action. So it proved tonight and though the deadlock lasted some minutes the fish kicked again, the line flicked away from whatever had caught it and the battle was back on. Briefly.

The fish powered off again and though I tightened the clutch and held on, after a few seconds everything went slack. It had straightened the hook.

I didn't feel too despondent at the time and tied on a bigger, stronger hook. I would surely get another chance.

Another hour passed before the rod-tip tweaked half an inch. I poised ready to strike. A minute ticked by, then another and suddenly everything went strange.

There was no tingling sensation, but instead a sharp shock up my spine which caused the hairs on my neck to stand up and my skin prickle. I spun round and knew that whatever or whoever was watching me was near a tree trunk around twenty yards behind my right shoulder. I have felt similar feelings before and since, and will often feel an urge to look skyward only to find a buzzard or hawk looking down on me, but this was an altogether different intensity that thumped my stomach like a bass drum. All thoughts of barbel and line tweaks vanished, displaced not by fear but more a state of hyper vigilance. I didn't have a torch but did have a lantern which I fumbled for, not wanting to look away from that tree trunk for a second. The lantern threw out its light, but merely made the shadowy undergrowth appear even more sinister, I would have to take the initiative for my own sanity. I grabbed a bank stick and the lantern and clomped loudly toward the trunk; there was nothing there.

I tried to fish on, breathing slowly to try and ease my nerves but I remained edgy and after twenty minutes or so that bolt of adrenaline shot through me once more and I felt again the malevolence coming from the same trunk behind me. I couldn't stay for another second and packed my gear away as quickly and loudly as possible, loading it on to my shoulders before pushing through the undergrowth.

The adrenaline was making easy work of the weight but had also left me disorientated, and twice I nearly walked straight into the river. The lantern was on but I had no spare hand to hold it and it swung from the handle of my rod bag scattering light but not showing me the way to safety. It was a panicky few minutes and I was imploring Martin to come and help me; he must surely be able to see the lantern from his position and realise that its scattering light meant I was having trouble. It turned out that he could see it, but watched the light spiralling around the trees willing me to get to him. He couldn't come to my aid because he was utterly frozen with fear.

When I finally reached Martin, despite the dark I could see his face had no colour left in it and he was in a mild state of shock. He had managed to pack most of his kit away, but had experienced the same fright as I had, though being out in the open had left him feeling even more exposed and the fear had actually made him physically sick. It was a tortuous walk back to the car, our nerves were still jangling and we were suffering from adrenaline comedown which leadened every footstep.

We talked little and Martin was asleep within minutes of setting off for home.

The following day saw us back on one of the familiar stretches; sharing the riverbank with other anglers didn't feel nearly so bad. I got chatting with one of them and mentioned where we had fished the evening before. He immediately raised his eyebrows and let out a nervous laugh.

"You won't see me down there again, mate," he said shaking his head. "Went down there last year with a mate and he came face to face with a big cat. We didn't hang around I can tell you."

There is a further postscript to this tale. The memory of that lost fish played on my mind and a few weeks later I summoned up the courage to make a return trip. It was daylight this time but that didn't stop the barbel feeding or a rather extraordinary encounter - but that is a story for another time.

Chapter Twelve

One Last Cast

Too much of a good thing can be wonderful.
MAE WEST

Before excess extraction turned her into a winterbourne, in those final few years when the eels and minnows would make their way upriver, the Candover Stream would throw up hatches all through the year. In such clean chalk filtered water, the sunlight would warm every stone and the white-clawed crayfish would jostle for cover alongside the caddis and freshwater shrimp.

The meadows that straddled the stream were a deep, lush green - perfect pasture for dairy cattle and too wet to ever claim as arable. The cries of lapwing and redshank would echo all year replaced at dusk by woodcock and the screech of the barn owl.

From April the sea of grass would be skimmed by wave after wave of swallows. House martins and the occasional swift would share the feast, but the meadows belonged to the swallows - certainly in my eyes. Five or six pairs would cram into the outbuildings in my parents' garden, a pattern shared throughout the valley. No shed was too small and the nests were incredibly productive. Most pairs would mange two broods in a season with an occasional third for the most fertile and frenetic parents. By August the electricity lines would sag as hundreds of swallows began to gather and it was this sight that I always used to dread seeing.

Swallows represented all that was positive. They arrived as the days were warming and as the school year became more tolerable. Summer term meant lunch breaks on the field and long evenings after homework. The teachers were smiling more too, though at the time I didn't realise it was for the very same reasons as the pupils. End of year exams were something of a dampener, but the prize beyond them was what we all craved. Six weeks of summer holiday.

With both parents teaching we were more fortunate than many kids who would have to attend summer camps or activity days back at the school that they had escaped. Six weeks is an awfully long time to the sponge-like mind of a child, but as soon as the swallows began to gather on those lines, I knew what was coming. In fairness, many of the first brood fledglings and non brooding parents would most likely have been gathering to roost on the telegraph lines through the summer, but with those long evenings I wouldn't have noticed. I'd have been back indoors and likely asleep before the sun had set. August is a peculiar month though. It lolls along quite nicely until the third week when everything seems to happen too fast. The combine harvesters have stripped all but a handful of fields back to stubble, the sticky humid evenings are giving way to dark, chilly starlit nights and the spectre of a new school year steps ever closer.

So much changes to the world in those six weeks of summer, but even more can change to a child. Reacquainting oneself to

One

friends who have grown three inches, lost teeth or gained a sun-tan can be an odd feeling, and dressed in a new blazer with that tie squeezing your neck is a discomfort you haven't missed for a second.

I would almost torment myself through the final week of the summer break; worrying far too much about what was coming rather than what was now. I tried to make every second count, but got too anxious about missing something and would often end up staring wistfully from a window and wondering where all the time was going.

The massing of swallows on the telegraph wires was a cloud that cast a shadow beyond the return to school of course. As the rows of birds thin to nothing so the long slog of winter grows ever closer and to a young angler this meant a decrease in the quality of sport and opportunity. I had read of autumn being the finest time of the year to be on the bank, but my local still-waters certainly didn't reflect that. The lily-pads on Alresford Pond would be browning and dying away and the tench would only feed sporadically. The water clarity increased but so too did that grey lifeless sheen on the surface. It wasn't until I began exploring running water that I realised that John Keats' season of 'mists and mellow fruitfulness' was very much a time for an angler to prosper by the water.

While fishing was such a perfect distraction from school and then work, I have always been wary of creating too great a con-trast between the two separate worlds. Rather as I spent the last hours of the school holidays mentally preparing for what lay ahead, so Sunday nights could be too great a strain to leave the river and immediately be considering a Monday morning. Worse still would be the cloud that would hang through the day, and soon I realised that Saturday was the better day to angle leaving Sunday to relax from the benefits. Though this made the journey home infinitely less foreboding, I soon learnt that whatever day I fished, I would always stall when it came to the final cast.

After the intensity of the witching hour, it can be hard to let the day go. You might be catching fish and not wanting the sport to end, or more often you have been taunted by opportunity as the light has faded and you know that another five minutes might just produce something special.

When anglers killed all they caught, there would, with fortune, be something to take home as a trophy at the end of the day. Evening talk would focus around the triumphs of the day, the battle won with the dinner that now sat upon the centre of the table. Fishing had that additional incentive.

For many years I, and almost all anglers, went nowhere without a keepnet which would provide similar reflection at the end of the day. Pulling in the net and admiring the day's catch (and showing it off) was a satisfying way to end the day. Modern angling sees little use for keepnets away from match-fishing but digital cameras can record a moment and give instant reminders when back at home.

The problem with a photograph though, is that it doesn't smell; it doesn't sing like the blackcap in the trees behind your shoulder; it doesn't give that same burst of excitement when striking, playing and netting the fish. It will capture a moment but not actually capture *the* moment, and it is a sense of *feeling* that an angler wants to prolong not the actual catching of fish.

That sense of connection that was felt with the first cast of the day is a painful one to break. Reeling in for a final time is a reminder of the constraints and structure with which time shackles us - that perpetual routine.

Many fisheries have rules determining when you have to leave the water. Often this will be 'an hour after sunset' which is essentially when it is too dark to fish, but some venues are a little more strict. My first trip to the Royalty stretch of the Avon was marred by the bailiff threatening to lock my car away for the night. I had taken the hour after sunset rule a little too liberally and not realised that a clock on the fishery was displaying the current 'sunset' to which I should have responded. Judging by the attitude of the bailiff I wasn't the first person to fall foul of local protocol.

One of my favourite venues is the Old Mill at Aldermaston. Prime water for barbel and chub. The Mill is a private residence and also caters for a variety of functions (Sue and I actually married there - in the close season of course), so while it offers one of the few day-ticket fishing opportunities on the Kennet, you are requested to pack up at seven o'clock.

In the summer this could be a frustration, especially on bright days when the barbel would keep their heads tucked into the weed-beds until the sun began to set. Come the autumn though, it could work very much in the angler's favour. Fishing around Christmas could be enjoyed two and a half hours into darkness, especially useful when targeting the chub.

With the stretch being popular as well as productive, the fish sometimes seemed to respond more to human time-keeping rather than the natural rhythm of the water. A lot of anglers would pack up fishless at around six-thirty, not realising that they were missing out on their best chance of the day. So often would I catch a good fish with my final cast that it was far more than just coincidence. Whether the fish were responding to the lack of angler presence or had learnt when they could feed more safely I'm not sure, but at any point in the season a tough day could be finished with a flourish at five to seven.

One autumn when the river was low after a dry summer, the Kennet seemed utterly lifeless during daylight, but my run of last minute fish continued. If Martin was with me he would pre-empt the bite, giving a word or whistle that it was that time of the day when I'd prove what a jammy bastard I was.

On another occasion I was just packing up when another angler wandered down the bank. He had been fishing one of my favourite chub swims but had not had a bite all day. As he headed off back towards the car park I had a quick glance at the time and saw I had five or six minutes of fishing time remaining. I had been on the brink of breaking down my rod but instead couldn't resist a quick cast in the chub hole. I managed two casts in the end, and had a big chub on each of them. The other angler was only just driving off as I arrived back at the car. He gave a quick wave but thankfully didn't chat - I was already feeling sheepish and didn't want to rub his nose in it.

A predetermined finish time does encourage a certain amount of panic, particularly within the physical process of casting. Knowing that there will be no time to tackle up again almost drives you to cast straight into the branches. A simple swing of a bait becomes the hardest task in the world.

I always cringe for those athletes making their final attempt in the long-jump or javelin, knowing that everything comes down to that moment. They will have been through the process a thousand times without a thought but now the intensity of the moment is all within their head. Golfers too, with a make or break shot, so dependent upon muscle memory and familiar method somehow have to treat the next swing as if it bears no consequence.

If you stop and think too much then you can forget everything. The javelin spears your big toe, the golf ball finds water and your final cast will wrap itself around that stray prickle of bramble that you hadn't even noticed was there.

Despite the propensity for disaster, the last cast of the day can so often be the most rewarding. In terms of connection, you will not have felt so sharp since your float first settled in the morning, and by this point of the day, if you have listened carefully then you know precisely where your bait has to be.

Alternatively, you can trust to luck or divine intervention, and this method is not without its successes. On one November trip to the Old Mill I had struggled against high, cold water and a biting wind. Despite the lack of daytime action I had been confident that darkness would bring a fish, but with time almost gone I had not had the slightest of knocks.

I had finished up in the main weirpool, fishing a lump of bacon grill in all of the areas of slack water where I had found fish in the past.

I put on a fresh chunk of meat for the final cast, but as I moved to swing it out so I realised that I was simply going through the motions. I had no belief that I would get a bite, and as I stopped for a moment and looked around the dark water below I had no faith that there would be a fish anywhere with a taste for bacon.

I looked skyward to see that the clouds, which had been thick all day, had parted directly above my head and in that split second a shooting star blazed across the gap.

Before any accusations come my way of spicing up a tale with a touch of Walt Disney, I should point out that this was mid-November when the Leonid meteor shower is at its most intense. Seeing a shooting star wasn't altogether surprising, though the timing of it (and the way it showed in the gap in the clouds) was an omen hard to ignore.

I looked back at the water in front of me and briefly saw the shape of a fish form in the choppy reflection of the weirpool. It was in the middle of the pool, a spot with no previous form, but I plonked my bait right on it and couldn't help but laugh as the line tweaked and tightened within seconds of the bait finding the bottom. It was possibly the finest conditioned barbel I have ever caught and though I treasured its capture and the quirks of fortune that led me to it, I was troubled on the way home by the despondency I felt moments before the meteor.

For whatever reason my focus had drifted. I was missing the beat somehow, listening to the same old tune when there were new melodies being played. It wasn't until the final cast that I realised my state of mind and then, thankfully, reacted to it.

The danger when fishing is to get preoccupied with the prize at the end of the chase, utter folly when Nature is your adversary as Captain Ahab found to his cost.

As he showed in the words of 'The Maldive Shark' poem, Hermann Melville was a man with a great appreciation of the natural world. In a time when so many attitudes were black and white, to present Ahab's relentless pursuit of Moby-Dick as an almost inevitably doomed obsession, was a demonstration that for all his intelligence and technology, Man's greatest failing will always be self induced. A failure to respect the sea and the creatures within it can only be to our own detriment, and the moment we lose our true sense of place, then so it becomes inevitable that we will lose everything.

Having unleashed his final harpoon into the great whale, Ahab tangles the cord around his own neck and as Moby-Dick dives down beneath the sinking wreckage of the ship, so he drags the captain to his death. After such a tumultuous battle through which Ishmael is the only man to survive, Melville closes his tale with a hint of indifference from the sea itself:

Now, small fowls flew screaming over the yet yawning gulf; a sullen white surf beat against its steep sides; the all collapsed, and the great shroud of the seas rolled on as it rolled five thousand years ago.

The voyage of the *Pequod* is filled with self discovery and perspective, an examination of God and social status; aspects that the crew and the reader view as fundamental to human nature. Yet through the wreck of it all, the sea continues to roll, constant and unaffected. Man can make a mark, he can score and burn and destroy but if he wants to involve, then he must work *with* the natural environment, not simply within it.

Ahab's final cast cost him his life, and though I wasn't really likely to have the same end on that November night on the Kennet, I would have left feeling empty had I not picked up the rhythm at the last, and not because I would have blanked. And of course the moment I stopped thinking about a need to catch a fish, so I promptly caught one.

Though they often produce fish, the more memorable last casts are so often those that do not. By packing away all but the rod and landing-net there is already a sense of detachment and this is an ideal moment to reflect upon the day and remind yourself of those sensations that have been most evocative.

At the final moment (because you are wearing a coat with cavernous pockets) you simply bite off the terminal tackle, stow your rod, shoulder your bag and head for home. All of the important aspects remain fresh as you walk - they have not been dissolved by the process of packing up as it is already done.

I spent a couple of evenings last autumn with Chris, fishing a lake with a rumoured population of true crucians. Both nights finished with memorable final casts but for very different reasons.

On the first, we fished well into dark with starlights glowing atop our floats. Chris had not used them before and was instantly addicted, especially as his float kept slipping under as a string of chunky roach found his breadflake bait.

I had been plagued by small rudd from the first cast, but as I made my last, so they finally seemed to have found their beds and the green glow of the float sat still on the edge of the lilies. I was on the brink of reeling in for the final time when the float dipped a fraction of an inch and I struck into a fish. It had to be a crucian and it proved to be a decent fish too, over two pounds. It was a lovely end to a lovely evening and a total contrast to the next when I headed for home with an even bigger smile.

We had struggled for bites but a tench apiece kept our hopes up. Whereas the previous evening had been cloudy and a little humid, tonight the sky was clear and the air had a nip to it that tickled our noses and clouded our breath. We both had radios in our bags, an item frowned upon (and even outlawed) on some banks, but essential if Southampton have got an evening kick-off. Tonight though, long after full-time, Chris crackled his radio to life in the pitch and found a concert just starting on Radio 3. It was a modern composer (I cannot recall who) and the music had an eerie resonance. I tuned my radio to the same frequency and we set them either side of us on a fairly low volume but with the music adding layers of atmosphere to the evening. We almost forgot about our original purpose, both sitting in our swims gazing skyward at the stars. A powerful spell was being cast and it was entirely fitting that the oblong shape of the International Space-Station should track across the black at that moment.

As the concert finished and the applause rippled across the lake's surface, we picked up our rods and floated back to the cars. I felt a sense of serenity on the drive home that evening which I would not possibly have felt had a fish interrupted my final cast, and it carried me through a sound night and well into a new day. It wasn't just the music that had lulled me so sweetly, but those notes had soothed my ears and given my other senses a chance to enjoy the balance within the darkness. Sometimes your hearing strains so hard to pick up the slightest sound that silence itself will buzz and fizz in your head like the hum from an electricity sub-station. Your other senses become drowned out by a sound that is not even real.

Running water can fill the void as well as any symphony and the tune is ever changing. Last winter I experienced the perfect final cast, and again I caught nothing from it.

My brother-in-law Ben had conducted some river monitoring surveys back in the autumn in his role with the Wiltshire Wildlife Trust. He specialises in invasive plant species and his catchment took him from the upper reaches of the Kennet and just over the border into Berkshire.

After his final day, he got talking to the river-keeper and after Ben's findings had been discussed they spoke of the fish and fishing on the estate. It is a strictly private stretch, but Ben could, if he wished, come and spend a day coarse fishing during the winter.

Ben was delighted, and so was I when he was invited to bring a friend.

It was late January when we made our trip and conditions were not good. Snow was falling as we pulled up beside the river which itself was high and coloured. I had tapped up Paul Smyth (who is something of a Kennet expert) for a few pointers as to where we might find some perch and it was his favourite pool to which we first headed.

One of the criss-crossing sidestreams split in two just above a copse and the left-hand arm tumbled through a small hatch before winding through the trees and back to the main river. Paul had found plenty of perch in the run-off of the hatch-pool, with a far-bank bush providing the hotspot. It certainly looked ideal, with the current nudging alongside a reed-bed before swirling into the bush. The floodwater was a problem though, and on the few occasions when I managed to work a bait in the right area it was dragged under by a stack of snags that had been washed in through the winter.

I made my way upstream to see how Ben was faring and was happy to hear that he had caught a chub on his second cast, though he too was now struggling in the conditions. We decided to work our way upstream. There had to be an area of kinder water, but having walked for half a mile we had not made a single cast. There was a bay on the far bank that looked inviting, but was impossible to fish from where we stood so we made our way to the very top of the fishery where we could cross over and work down the other bank. It was a wasted venture. The bay was far too shallow to hold many fish, and though a sea-trout gave me my first bite of the day it took around an hour to pick a safe route back out of the flooded meadow and on to firmer riverbank.

Lunchtime came and went, and though we were loving the location and one another's company, we were aching to find a nice near-bank slack where we could let a float sit unmolested from the flow.

By mid-afternoon we had fished our way back to the cars and decided to continue downstream. A small cut-off offered us hope of a perch, but we searched every inch without the slightest hint of a bite. I did pick up another sea-trout from the crease formed where the carrier met the main river but we were running out of ideas.

Paul had mentioned a weed-rack at the bottom end of the fishery which had produced perch in the past. The long walk had put us off up until now, but we decided that with nowhere else offering much hope we may as well walk the mile and a half and at least see how the water was looking around the rack.

With the sky already bruising we avoided the temptation of any pools en route and walked briskly around the long sweeping bend that led us down towards the rack. To our right was a vast floodplain alive with waterfowl, teal particularly abundant, while the less moist meadows beyond the far bank were throbbing with snipe. There was a wonderful sense of desolation about the landscape, though having been happily losing ourselves within the wilderness our hopes of a perch waned quickly as we reached the weed-rack itself.

The rack had been replaced - very recently by the look of things, and the river thundered unchecked through the frame of the new barrier. Having walked this far and with the light fading, we decided to at least have one cast in the area, and a little way back upstream found a run of quieter water beneath a couple of alders.

I gathered some fuel together for the kettle and lowered a worm alongside a small weed-bed beneath my feet. There was around four feet of water and a small bush was deflecting the current far enough into the main body that my float sat almost still behind it.

Ben, a little further upstream, gave a quick whistle. He wasn't into a fish, but was pointing behind us where a barn owl was quartering the tussocks just forty yards away. I smiled. This would do just nicely. We watched the owl work closer towards us before it made an unsuccessful grab at something and worked off upriver. I turned to find my float had gone and lifted the rod in almost disbelief to find a fish on the end.

It was a perch, and a pretty good one of two and a quarter pounds. The kettle hadn't even boiled yet and already this spot had delivered far more than I had hoped. There was time for another fish too, and I urged Ben to join me - perch rarely swim alone.

Within a couple of minutes my float dipped again but I was too fast on the strike and bumped off a good fish. The kettle was beginning to steam and I readied the mugs and was just about to pour the water when I noticed Ben lifting his rod sharply. The bend in the tip suggested he had connected with something, but so cold was the water that the fish didn't respond until it hit the surface. It rolled and in that moment I gulped - it was a perch and it had to be a 3-pounder.

I didn't want to panic Ben so bit my lip and worked the landing-net into position. The perch made a lazy dive for the main channel but didn't have the oomph and Ben calmly turned it and drew it towards the bank and into the net.

It was a clonking fish, thickset and, but for a slight deformity in the dorsal, scale and fin-perfect. The needle on the scales flickered a fraction below 3lb 12oz so we settled on 3.11 and a half - Ben's biggest perch by a country mile, though I was competing with him in the race to wear the broadest smile.

And then came the best bit of the day. As the perch sunk back into the river, I poured the tea and we stood, mugs in hand, grinning at one another. I made a token last cast, having slid off the float which I could no longer see and feeling the line for a bite.

No bite would come, and nor did I really want one; another fish could not have completed the day any more than it already was.

It didn't matter that Ben had caught the beast, in fact it seemed rather fitting that the river had rewarded him for the work he did in her cause. The final smudges of daylight vanished with our last sips of tea - a mug has never tasted finer.

And as we crunched our way back upstream we rode on a wave of contentment. Ben was smiling. I knew though I could not see his face. He simply had to be. He would be beaming as I was.

Still I smile, remembering the feelings as I write these words. And as I recollect the day, I don't actually recall reeling in. I must have done for the rod I was using is standing in the hall, but when a day ends as well you don't actually stop fishing.

We will always dream of fishes, and catching them, but deeper still is that sense of serenity; of wholeness. The casts we make in our sleep are every bit as real as the ones we make beside the river, because they keep us connected. Connected with the streams that flow within our selves.

Acknowledgements

Big thanks to Tom Hodgkinson, Dan Kieran and Gavin Pretor-Pinney for making me an Idler and allowing me to continue Idling.

Thanks to Rose and Jon Ward-Allen at Medlar for their support and for giving so much to Angling Literature.

To all the people I have fished with - too many to name, but special mention to my father Geoff, brother Richard, late grandfather Dennis, Martin Stevens, Chris Yates, Ben Fitch, Hugh Ortega-Breton, Leapy Leigh, Peter Arlott, Jon Berry, Kieran Topping, Jules and Nell Gibson, Lawrence Pointer, Steve Dance, Chris Semple and Andy Maple.

To my family for their support, Cath and Ben for their unending encouragement, Chris and Dan as ever, and the finest fishing widow an angler could ever wish to marry, Sue.

Sources

Applin, Arthur, *Philandering Angler*, Hurst and Blackett, 1942.

Barker, Thomas, *The Art of Angling or Barker's Delight*, R. Marriot, 1651.

Barnes, Julian, *A History of the World in 10½ Chapters*, Jonathan Cape, 1989.

Francis, Francis, *A Book on Angling* 4th Edition, Longmans, Green and Co., 1876.

Grahame, Kenneth, *The Wind in the Willows*, Methuen, 1908.

Grey, Sir Edward, *Fly Fishing*, JM Dent, 1899.

Hughes, Ted, *Poetry in the Making*, Faber and Faber, 1967.

Irving, Washington, *The Sketch Book of Geoffrey Crayon, Gent. No. 1*, CS Van Winkle et al, c1820.

MacLean, Norman, *A River Runs Through It*, University of Chicago Press, 1976.

Melville, Herman, *John Marr and Other Sailors*, Privately Published, 1899

Melville, Herman, *Moby Dick*, Harper and Brothers, 1851.

O'Gorman, James, *The Practice of Angling*, William Curry, Jun. and Company, 1845.

Paxman, Jeremy, *Fish, Fishing and the Meaning of Life*, Penguin, 1995.

Pepys, Samuel, *The Joys of Excess*, Penguin, 2011.

Ransome, Arthur, *The Picts and the Martyrs*, Jonathan Cape, 1943.

Ransome, Arthur, *Rod and Line*, Jonathan Cape, 1929.

Shakespeare, William, *Hamlet,* Ling and Trundell, 1603.

Shelley, Mary, *Frankenstein,* Colburn and Bentley, 1831 edition.

Sheringham, H. T., *Coarse Fishing,* Adam and Charles Black,1912.

Sheringham, H. T., *Trout Fishing: Memories and Morals,* Hodder and Stoughton, 1920.

Thoreau, Henry David, *Walden or Life in the Woods*, Ticknor and Fields, 1854.

Walton, Izaak, *The Compleat Angler,* R. Marriot, 1653.

White, Gilbert, *The Natural History of Selborne*, White, Cochrane and Co, 1789.

Wordsworth, William, *Poems in Two Volumes*, Longman, Hurst, Rees, and Orme, 1807.

Yates, Chris, *Nightwalk*, Collins, 2012.

BassMaster.com
Birdwatching Magazine
medstead.org
IsleofEigg.net

With a nod to Wikipedia, hearsay and the greatest storytellers of all, the anglers.